Shaman
in Disguise

Shaman
in Disguise

Wendy Taylor

BOOKS

Winchester, UK
Washington, USA

First published by O-Books, 2010
O Books is an imprint of John Hunt Publishing Ltd., The Bothy, Deershot Lodge, Park Lane, Ropley,
Hants, SO24 0BE, UK
office1@o-books.net
www.o-books.com

Distribution in:

UK and Europe
Orca Book Services Ltd
Home trade orders
tradeorders@orcabookservices.co.uk
Tel: 01235 465521
Fax: 01235 465555

Export orders
exportorders@orcabookservices.co.uk
Tel: 01235 465516 or 01235 465517
Fax: 01235 465555

USA and Canada
NBN
custserv@nbnbooks.com
Tel: 1 800 462 6420 Fax: 1 800 338 4550

Australia and New Zealand
Brumby Books
sales@brumbybooks.com.au
Tel: 61 3 9761 5535 Fax: 61 3 9761 7095

Far East (offices in Singapore, Thailand,
Hong Kong, Taiwan)
Pansing Distribution Pte Ltd
kemal@pansing.com
Tel: 65 6319 9939 Fax: 65 6462 5761

South Africa
Stephan Phillips (pty) Ltd
Email: orders@stephanphillips.com
Tel: 27 21 4489839 Telefax: 27 21 4479879

Text copyright Wendy Taylor 2009

ISBN: 978 1 84694 434 5

Design: Stuart Davies

A CIP catalogue record for this book is available
from the British Library.

Printed in the UK by CPI Antony Rowe, Chippenham

Disclaimer
Some names have been changed at the authors request.

O Books operates a distinctive and ethical publishing philosophy in
all areas of its business, from its global network of authors to
production and worldwide distribution.

CONTENTS

Bibliography
Dr. Eve Bruce   Shaman MD
Simon Buxton   The Shamanic Way of the Bee
Lewis Carroll   The Walrus and the Carpenter
Michael J. Harner   The Way of the Shaman
Carl Gustav Jung.   Synchronicity
Mathew Manning   The Link
James Arevalo Mevejildo   The Awakening of the Puma
John Perkins   Shapeshifting.
Michael Willis   Tibet

Chapter 1

THE JOURNEY BEGINS

It was the first of August 1990 and a beautiful sunny morning. The day had started the same as any other. There was nothing to indicate that it would be singularly different from the conservative pattern of each day – no prior warning that I was on the brink of events that would dramatically change my life forever.

My life at that time epitomized the Ultimate Dream. On a superficial level it appeared perfect, for I was surrounded by everything our culture is taught to seek, everything we are conditioned to believe will bring happiness. The home where I sat gazing out of the windows was a glorious medieval manor house, surrounded by a water-filled moat. It had twenty rooms, many containing beautiful antique furniture.

Outside, there was a heated swimming pool, a tennis lawn, formal grounds and an old, walled kitchen garden. A path through the orchard led to a small lake full of koi, and beyond this was our private woodland where a stream ran through – home to a pair of kingfishers – and wild deer wandered freely.

Our three horses grazed all day in fenced paddocks. At night they resided in stables facing the square cobbled courtyard behind the house, just outside my back door.

It was indeed a perfect setting. And at the end of the long graveled driveway the road gave fast access to major towns for marathon shopping trips and good restaurants.

My husband was a very successful company director; we traveled first class, stayed in the best hotels around the world and had top-of-the-line cars. Our three children had been privately educated and were now grown. Although they often still came 'home' for meals and returned occasionally to live under our roof for short spells, they were for the most part independent.

I had always been a stay-at-home mother who had given my family priority, so once the children left I was determined to find new interests and take advantage of my freedom. I was fit and considered myself of reasonable intelligence. Feeling the need to prove myself, I enrolled at the local flying school, overcame many fears, completed the training, passed the tests and gained a private pilot's license. My belief in my ability to achieve what I set out to do was verified, but strangely this brought no sense of fulfillment.

Now what? Here was the lifestyle I had dreamed of and strived for. I was living it! I should have been ecstatic, but I wasn't; in fact I was unhappier than I had ever been in my life. There was an emptiness. I felt hollow and I couldn't understand why.

The last few months had been difficult. My marriage had been through a bad patch and my children all had personal problems. Previous to that, I had needed a mastectomy. These could have been factors in my unhappiness, but I wasn't dwelling on them and felt they were problems that could be resolved.

My sense of isolation and pain was welling up from somewhere deeper. Indeed pain and isolation had been my companions long before the onset of the current situation. The role of 'corporate wife' had never been one in which I felt comfortable – it was play-acting – and for years there had been a growing sense that I should be doing more with my life.

But what?

Dawning on me was the realization that material wealth did not guarantee happiness. The effort expended to achieve all of these trappings seemed pointless. Where was the joy? I loved my family deeply; I loved the animals in my care; but there seemed no purpose to my life. I had fulfilled my role as a wife and mother, and had proved I was still capable of embarking on other areas and being successful. But what now? What was I looking for? How could I fill this void?

It was in these idyllic surroundings and in this frame of mind that I stood in front of the mirror that summer morning. Powerful events were about to commence, events that would irrevocably change my life. Unknown to me at the time, this moment was to be the start of a personal 'shape-shift'. Mysticism does not restrict itself to fundamentalists or those searching for it. Sometimes it enters into the lives of those innocents who are totally unaware of other dimensions.

It was 10.00am. My husband was at his office in London. The house was empty apart from me and the dogs. Earlier I had attended to the horses; I was now showered and in front of the mirror, putting on my make-up.

This is where it becomes difficult to tell precisely what happened next. Metaphysical experiences have been deemed unacceptable in our society for so many years that the language for describing such happenings has long ago been lost.

As I stood there, a 'knowing' that a burglary was going to take place later in the day came into my head. It shocked me with its clarity, for in that instant I was convinced it was my cousin's house that was the target of the crime. I turned from the mirror, picked up a scrap of paper and a pen, and wrote, 'Time is 10.00am. Joyce's home will be burgled today.'

This thought had arrived without warning or preconception. It wasn't a subject I had been discussing; there had been no such occurrences around me; and this cousin was not a member of the extended family whom I saw very often.

Then I became concerned. I was positive that the thought was real, and the need to warn her became an issue. But when exactly would the burglary happen? Could I prevent it? I sat down, staring at the words that were written on the notepaper. The intensity of 'knowing' was starting to ease and I went back to complete my make-up.

I carried the knowledge of this predestined event around with me all day. Although I failed to do anything constructive about it, the message was at the forefront of my thoughts as the hours continued through their normal routine. That evening, I showed the scrap of paper to my husband and tried to convey the overwhelming awareness and sense of urgency that had accompanied the written thought. He listened, but was uninterested and with a shrug of the shoulders dismissed the notion.

The next morning I was still puzzling over it, when the phone rang. I answered it and recognized the voice; it was Liz, my hairdresser, who came to my home every three weeks to attend to my hair.

'I'm so sorry, Wendy,' she said. 'I was due to visit you this morning, but I won't be able to come. My house was broken into last night and I have to remain in today as the police are coming back. But if you want to come over to my home, I'll do your hair here.'

I thanked her and agreed to do just that. She gave me her address and route directions, and I replaced the receiver. As I put the phone down, I stood there staring at it, feeling very confused. Then I looked at the clock and saw the time, and the hairs on my arms stood up – it was precisely 10.00am. It had been exactly this time yesterday that I had received that powerful intuition. The burglary had indeed happened, just as I had foreseen. The only difference was that I had misinterpreted the victim – it was my hairdresser, not my cousin. But in that instant it dawned on me that my cousin's surname is Head.

How strange! It seemed that I had picked up a definite message. But where had it come from? I was more puzzled than ever.

It was about a twenty-minute drive to Liz's home. As I neared the area, I suddenly felt odd – not unwell, but there was a definite change in awareness. It was a condition that I would become accustomed to in the weeks ahead and come to recognize as a shift in consciousness. Right now, I had to cope with vivid pictures flooding into my head.

I pulled the car into the side of the road; the images were holding my attention, and they were so strong and distracting it was impossible to drive. It was as if a giant television set had been placed directly in front of my eyes, gripping my visual senses. The pictures appearing were clear, sharp and in full color. I saw a man and a child.

The man had a gypsy-like appearance with swarthy skin and dark curly hair. He looked to be in his middle thirties; he was of average height and stockily built. My attention was drawn to his clothes: he was wearing a crumpled dark suit and what I felt was a dirty shirt, but at odds with the suit were the scruffy and well-worn trainers on his feet. There was a sense that a suit was not this man's usual attire.

The child was a young boy who in stark contrast was blond, fair-skinned and about three to four years old. I didn't register what he was wearing, but a vivid red scratch on the left-hand side of his neck was discernible.

The two were standing side by side on the pavement, looking at a house. As I continued to watch, the man took the child by the hand and walked quickly through the gateway and along the path by the side of the house. At a point before he reached the back of the building, he stopped, then bent over and picked the child up. There was a small transit window on the side of the house which was slightly ajar and through this gap the man pushed the child in, head first.

I watched this action in amazement, sensing with an unquestionable certainty that I was watching a replay of the uninvited entry into Liz's home. The picture faded. Blinking hard, I pulled out back into the stream of traffic and continued the short distance to my destination.

When I arrived, Liz showed me through to the rear of the house and we walked into her conservatory. I had a lightheaded feeling, somewhat dreamlike.

'We'll do your hair here,' she said.

I sat down and commiserated with her at the invasion of her home.

'Fortunately, there was no damage and they didn't take much,' she replied, sounding quite relieved. 'They seem to have concentrated on our bedroom. Drawers were opened and had been looked through. They took some money and jewelry from my bedside table, but they also stole my husband's passport. Now that *has* caused a problem as he was due to fly to America tomorrow.'

She placed a towel around my shoulders, and as she did so, I glanced up.

'That's where they got in!' I exclaimed, pointing to one of the small windows. I then proceeded to share with her what I had seen on my personal 'television screen'.

'Well, that's very strange,' she answered, 'but no, I don't think so. The police came after we got in last night and seemed to think it was two men and they had probably gained access through the front door.'

I said no more, but I knew differently.

A few minutes later, her husband Eric put his head around the door. 'Liz? The fingerprint guy is here. He wants to check this room. Is it okay for him to come in?'

'Do you mind, Wendy?' she asked of me.

I raised no objection and the detective entered. He nodded in our direction and then commenced dusting surfaces with his brush and powder. He soon became engrossed in his own task and Liz continued attending to my hair.

Suddenly the detective looked across at us, and directing his question at Liz, said, 'Excuse me; do you have any small children?' Liz responded in the negative – she has no children of her own. He then asked, 'Have there been any visiting recently?'

After a few seconds' thought, Liz volunteered, 'Well, my niece was here last week, but she's nearly twelve.'

The detective shook his head. 'No, that's not it. Here, look at this.' And he pointed at a pane of glass. There, plainly visible in the white dust, were several tiny handprints. What was astonishing was that they were all upside down.

He stood holding his pot and brush, looking at the evidence. 'That's where the culprit gained access. A small child has been put through that little window above this large fixed pane. It looks as if someone outside must have held the child by the ankles until their hands reached the sill. Would you believe it!'

Liz looked at him; her jaw dropped and her mouth opened. She called Eric in and said, 'Wendy. Tell them what you've just told me.'

I repeated the story, trying to make light of it. The logical part of my mind was hoping they wouldn't think I was somehow implicated; there was also a hovering fear that I was being sucked into something way beyond my control.

Eric stood quietly listening. 'Well,' he added, 'that would explain why all the drawers of the tall chest in our bedroom were opened except for the two top ones!'

The detective had also been listening intently. He conveyed his thanks, and without passing further comment tidied his utensils and departed.

Soon afterwards, satisfied with my hairstyle, I was on my way home. What was happening? Where was this information coming from? The questions went round and round in my head. This sort of thing didn't happen to people like me. I was an 'everyday' housewife, not some flowing-robed mystic.

Before I had driven far, a repetition of the 'wave' of energy engulfed me. It felt similar to receiving a mild electric shock and it jumped my consciousness onto another level. Once again I started to 'see'. This time it was a crone-like figure, clothed in black with a long, thin, ancient face and prominent hooked nose – the archetypal witch. It was a frightening sight and appeared directly in front of me, almost obliterating my vision.

I slowed the car right down, pulled into the side, and mentally started demanding that the apparition leave. There was a strangely telepathic communication; I was insisting that it leave, but also agreeing that it could return if it waited until I got home. I also found myself making the strange action of repeatedly rolling my lower lip outwards and over.

The vision cleared. Now that I could pay attention to the traffic, I continued my drive home. However, I remained very aware that the hag-like figure was lurking close by.

I pulled up outside my house and leapt out of the car, fairly running for the door. Once inside the kitchen, I grabbed a sheet of paper and a pen, and as I sat down at the table it was as if an outside force had taken over my body. My hand started to write very quickly. For a few minutes this energy consumed me, like a fire ripping through me, before it suddenly departed. It was the strangest sensation – not as if it had burnt out, but rather as if I had been in the path of a tornado that had come from nowhere and swept me up, then dropped me as it moved on.

My consciousness had returned to a normal level. I surveyed the paper in front of me: some of the writing was barely legible. I had been an instrument, for the words were not motivated or initiated by my mind and it was barely recognizable as my handwriting. I read what I had written.

The first words were clear:

> sorrow
> argument
> Irish

Underneath these was written:

> somebody still has the passport
> who has the passport

can I get the passport

Further down the page was:

police will arrest for another offense
he will have the passport on him
few days
The final words read:
they only wanted the passport

Around this last statement, the pen had drawn rings seven times.

In a little over twenty-four hours my life had been turned upside down. It was all quite bizarre. This *energy* which enveloped me – the closest word I could find to describe it – left me feeling as if I was being plugged into a power source, but a power that defied description. I went to the mirror and stared into it, not sure what I was expecting to see: the reflected image looked no different from the one I normally saw. However, I found myself looking deeply into my eyes. For a split second, there was a depth I had never been aware of before; for a fleeting moment I felt that I knew everything, that everything made sense and had a purpose.

Calling the dogs, I walked out into the garden. Many times, when there were problems to solve and emotional wounds to heal, I would turn to the animals. A meander through sunlit fields with the dogs, or a ride on my horse in the wind and rain, would always ease the pain and clear my vision. But today I was provided with no answers, only more questions.

Somehow I was being used. My physical body was providing a channel for someone or something. I was beginning to accept this, yet somehow there was no fear and I realized that at no time had I totally refused to comply – maybe refusal wasn't an option. Bewildering as it all was, I stood in awe.

I returned to the house. Several times I read through what

had been written, then I picked up the phone and called Liz. I didn't go into detail about what had occurred; I simply referred to it as 'a thought' and recommended that she call the detective handling the investigation and suggest to him that it might have been solely the passport the thieves were after and that the culprit might possibly be Irish.

'Well, Wendy,' she said, 'it didn't occur to me until after you had left, but almost surely you were right about the child. And the fingerprints would seem to confirm it. This would explain about the drawers. There's a tall chest in my bedroom, and all of the drawers had been opened except the top two. That could be the reason; a small child wouldn't have been able to reach that high. It's all so horrid – not just the upset of having your home violated but the inconvenience of it all. Eric has an American passport so he's had to travel up to London to try and sort it out at the embassy. Please let me know if anything else transpires.'

It was in a dreamlike state that I turned my attention to more mundane matters. My body moved into automatic as I prepared the evening meal, whilst the day's events continued to course through my head. I was anxious for my husband to return, as I desperately need to share all of this with someone else. His occupation as CEO of a multinational company was intense and stressful, but he was intelligent and capable. However, what he would make of this was anybody's guess. How do you apply logic to such a phenomenon?

Barry had barely got through the door before I started to describe the day's events. I followed him around as he changed out of his suit and poured himself a drink. He looked at me quizzically. 'Calm down,' he said. 'Just wait and see if it happens again.'

Although this wasn't what I wanted to hear, it was probably sound advice. At that point in our lives, we were absorbed in the physical realm. We were both very materialistic and great consumers. Any suggestion that a non-physical realm existed would have been met with incredulity and dismissed out of hand. Even so, being told to calm down was an instruction difficult to maintain, for I felt like a coiled spring. I urgently needed someone to explain what was going on.

No explanation was forthcoming. I felt quite helpless as there was not a thing I could do. Who do you phone?

However, before the evening ended, Barry was to witness a bout of this spontaneous outburst of abnormal behavior. This time, I sensed a shift in the energy of the room; I felt it arrive before it actually touched me.

We were sitting in the study, peacefully watching TV, when I shouted, 'It's coming again!' and jumped to my feet.

'Sit down!' Barry commanded. 'And calm down! What *is* it?' He was very angry. For him, being out of control is almost a crime.

'The energy – it's happening again!' I shouted.

This time, there was a witness, an observer of what was happening. But trying to describe the sensation I was experiencing was impossible. My body was vibrating and my head was filling with images that claimed priority. I turned my attention to the pictures that were forming. As I received them, I verbalized the scenes. Again I was experiencing the inexplicable: vivid, moving pictures were filling my head.

I was seeing, as clearly as if he had been standing in the room, a close male friend of ours named David. He was looking very distressed. Then I saw a hospital – to be precise, I saw a large building that I *knew* was a hospital. Next I was aware of Catherine, his wife – that she was very ill. I felt a great sense of urgency.

The whole episode lasted, as before, less than a couple of minutes but was of overwhelming intensity. Like a cyclone moving through, it had momentarily sucked me in, and as it passed on, normality once more returned. 'Curiouser and curiouser'. I *knew* without question that the scene that had been shown to me was at that very moment being enacted elsewhere in the country, but there was nothing else I could do to throw any more light on this latest excursion into the metaphysical.

It had been a mysterious but exhausting day. With a certain reluctance I went to bed, but before long I was once more awake. As I lay there, I was aware that something had awoken me. Then I heard it.

It was a voice in my head, saying, 'Wake up!' It was an androgynous voice, and the two words were conveyed as an order. 'Wake up. Wake up now!' it repeated.

My senses were alerted. I propped myself up in bed and, still feeling half asleep, reached out my hand and put on the bedside light. The instruction continued further: 'Switch on the television.'

Without questioning, I did so. As the television sprang to life I focused my eyes on the screen. There were mutterings and objections from the other side of the bed, but the voice that only I was hearing overruled them.

The commercial break that intersperses each show was in full flow. An advert for an insurance company was flashing through a series of potential household accidents, focusing on faulty electrical appliances; it concluded by showing a large light bulb exploding. Somehow I was aware that there was a connection with my youngest son. There was no concern on my part, however; I knew there was no need to worry. Even though my sleep had been disturbed, it was nothing serious.

I switched off the TV, put out the light and attempted to return to sleep, but my head was buzzing with thoughts.

My background was Irish Catholic but I had long ago given up going to mass or attending any Christian church, for the patriarchal beliefs of all Western religions were at odds with my feelings that God did not harbor preferences. My education had been at convent schools where the nuns had used fear as a means of instilling discipline and keeping control – again something that I instinctively felt was not advocated by a Higher Power.

I held on to a belief in guardian angels, in a non-human figure that watches over each of us. Perhaps this stemmed from an early memory of a picture that used to hang in my grandmother's house. It showed a child reaching out over a perilous ledge to pick a flower; by her side was a luminous being, with powerful white-feathered wings, standing as protection, ready to catch her should she fall. Maybe these communications were emanating from such beings, but as yet I had seen none.

Another order came. The voice said, 'Write it down!'

There was no way of ignoring it so I put the light back on, picked up a pen and paper, and wrote down the details of the advertisement I had watched. I noted the time and added it: '1.20am'. The voice seemed to have gone now and I was free to return to sleep.

Morning dawned and I entered the day with a mixture of anticipation and apprehension. The abnormal happenings started as soon as I picked up the newspaper: the knowledge of every major story contained within it flashed through my head before I had even glanced at the front page. I hurriedly flipped through; it was all there. This was an incredible sensation. How did I know all of this? And how could I possibly expect anyone to believe me and accept it? The day had only just started and already I had to face a bagful of mixed emotions.

As soon as I had a moment to myself, I sat down at the kitchen table with the dogs lying at my feet and wrote down every detail of these extraordinary happenings. I recorded the date and times, and the difficulty of finding words to accurately describe the intensity of both the physical and emotional sensations I was experiencing. I even wrote down what the weather was like and what I was eating, for there was a deep-down fear that if the situation escalated I might be considered mentally unbalanced, in which case this would be a record for the doctor.

I questioned whether the cause was menopausal. Did I have a

tumor in my head? Was I going mad? The biggest question of all was, *Why me?* It was frightening, for I knew I was walking a fine line between what our culture defines as sanity and insanity. I was aware that I was balancing precariously somewhere in-between.

Two telephone calls later in the day convinced me that I was not mentally deranged, but that some outside force was directing me, a force completely beyond my comprehension. The first call was from me to my youngest son, Daniel. He was living away from home in his first attempt at independence, sharing a house with three of his contemporaries. Without preliminaries, I went straight to the point.

'Dan, did you have an accident last night?' I asked.

'No, Mum,' he said, immediately on the defensive before a questioning mother.

'Are you sure?' I persisted, continuing my line of inquiry. 'Nothing major – perhaps just an accident in the house?'

'Well, there was something,' he admitted. 'We were watching TV and the reception wasn't very good, so while the commercials were on, Tony had a fiddle with the electrics. I didn't touch it.' (Having grown up as the youngest of three, he was well-practiced at covering his quarters.) 'I went into the kitchen,' he continued, 'and was getting a bottle of milk out of the fridge when there was a huge bang and all the electrics blew. I dropped the bottle of milk, which smashed, making a bit of a mess... but nobody was hurt and we sorted it out. Is that what you're talking about?' I carried on listening while this young man voiced his priorities. 'It was a shame because now the TV isn't working any more and we were watching a good film that I didn't get to see the end of.'

As an afterthought, I posed another question. 'What time did all this happen?'

'Oh, late,' he muttered. 'Must have been getting on for 1.30am.'

Sons invariably grow up accepting that mothers often mysteriously seem to know what they are up to, and Daniel seemed happy to let the subject drop. After hearing that he would be over to see me later in the day, I said goodbye. However, before I had even moved from the spot, I rang him back.

'Be careful as you drive out from your parking place,' I told him. Something from the episode in the night was registering and there was a feeling he would break the headlight of his car.

Later that afternoon, he turned up and volunteered to help out for a couple of hours; with a place the size of ours there was always a lot to do. Even through the summer, on chilly days we would have a big log fire, so I sent him down into one of the barns where the dead tree branches from our woodland were stacked, and he set about chopping some wood.

A short while later, he came looking for me. 'Sorry, Mum,' he said. 'Had a bit of an accident. One of the pieces of wood that I chopped somehow flew across, ricocheted up, and smashed the big light in the barn.'

I was amazed. It was not one hundred percent correct but the prediction was close enough and made me very happy.

The second surprise came shortly afterwards: an incoming phone call from Barry.

'You're never going to believe this,' I heard him say, 'but I've just spoken to David.' (This was the friend I had 'seen' in the vision the previous evening.) He continued, 'He called to tell me about Catherine. Apparently yesterday, while they were at their home in Devon, she was in dreadful pain. He called the doctor who immediately rushed her off to hospital for an emergency operation. She had an ectopic pregnancy – all very scary – and they operated in the evening. Thankfully all is well now. The worst is over and she's expected to make a full recovery.'

This confirmation of my clairvoyance from the previous evening was wonderfully reassuring, but again raised endless questions.

Throughout the following days, similar notions would randomly, but daily, enter my head, always fractionally preceded by the familiar shift in awareness as the only warning. They simply arrived and interrupted whatever I was doing. Sometimes they came as dreams but with an extra vividness; I would remember these with clarity as I woke up, knowing they were somehow special.

One such dream was of two planes colliding. The larger plane made an emergency safe landing, but the smaller plane had been clipped on the wing and crashed, killing both occupants. The terrain was shown to me in detail, along with the wreckage and part of the registration letters. On television the following day, this accident was reported; the news showed film of the debris and focused on the call-sign letters on the damaged body of the craft which were identical to those I had recorded from my dream.

Another time, I was again awoken in the night by the insistent voice in my head saying, 'Wake up, wake up!'

I really didn't want to and bizarrely I answered it: 'I *am* awake', to which the response was, 'Wake up properly. Sit up and put the light on.'

I struggled to open my eyes, but sat up and swung my legs over the side of the bed. This time there was no surge of energy and no instruction to switch on the television. I looked around the room. It was my bedroom, no different from how it always had been. On semi-automatic, I picked up the pad and pen and wrote the time: '3.30am'.

What am I doing? I thought. *What am I supposed to write down?* I sat there, knowing I had been awoken to do something. But what? This one I had to work out for myself. There was an innate 'knowing' that there was something to do and there was no point in rolling back into bed.

On the duvet lay part of a newspaper, a page where Barry had abandoned a half-completed crossword. There was a small picture of Madonna – not the Virgin Mary but the pop star. Next to where I had written the time, I added, 'A picture of Madonna. Looks like Marilyn Monroe.'

Still sitting there, feeling like a schoolchild unable to complete her homework, I wrote a few more words: '3.40am: Is this a lesson? Am I being dumb?', then found myself underlying the word 'dumb'.

The notes continued: '4.00am: Went down to the kitchen to make a cup of tea.' On returning to the bedroom, I added another cryptic sentence: 'Will be in the news soon.' And yet a few more words: 'Just have to say goodbye.'

It dawned on me that this was something to do with Marilyn Monroe, whom some called 'the dumb blonde', but I could get nothing positive so simply added the time and a final sentence: '4.30am: The precise time is important.' I then fell back to sleep.

My first thoughts on waking were on trying to justify how I had spent sixty minutes in the early hours puzzling out why the name of a long-dead film star was preventing me from sleeping. Before I did anything else that morning, I started to search through our reference and biography books. I soon found what I was looking for.

Today was the anniversary of Marilyn Monroe's demise. This discovery gave me goose bumps, but it was when I read the biography section of that day's *Daily Telegraph* that I was stunned. The article not only stated that this was the twenty-eighth anniversary of her passing but added that the doctors had noted her death as occurring sometime between 3.30am and 4.30am – exactly the hour I had been awake.

But why had I been woken up to note this? It was quite fascinating but impossible to understand, and it also seemed rather pointless.

Mentally I was walking a tightrope; to onlookers nothing about me had changed. Somehow I was coping with routine domestic chores and social events, but it was like existing in two realities, for in my head I was living twenty-four hours ahead of the rest of the world. This ability to see into the future was disturbing, because constantly I was being shown very painful scenes.

One instance was of a man drowning while trying to retrieve his dog from a water-filled quarry. This time, I recorded the name of the small market town where he lived, which was not many miles away, and the breed of the dog. Twenty-four hours later, our local paper corroborated this fact and gave further details of this sad event.

The understanding that I was unable to prevent or change anything was hard to handle. Although thankfully I was never shown anything of this nature that related directly to family or friends, it was still emotionally distressing. It was a lonely and frightening time. I kept these continuing incidents to myself, sharing them with no one, and there dwelt within me a constant awareness of the narrow line I was walking and of the need to keep my life in balance. I had learned very quickly that dimensions existed beyond my normal perception and learned also to keep quiet about this new discovery.

Chapter 2

CHAIN OF CONNECTIONS

A greater understanding of these mystic realms, and a sense of compatibility with them, would, for me, remain in the distant future. For the present, the 'voice' was constantly with me and even more drama was yet to unfurl. I found myself in an unbelievable situation as events concerning the burglary started to gather speed and the connection with Liz was reinforced.

Less than a week had passed since the commencement of these inexplicable happenings. The day had gone by without any input – but I felt 'strange'. It was like standing out on the plains feeling the wind increase and watching the storm clouds gather around me. There was a sense of power collecting.

I climbed into bed that night half-expecting another input from the unseen power source. My senses felt on red alert. Barry was watching the remainder of a television program as he sat in bed. I put my book aside and snuggled down ready for sleep, but it was not to be. This time it was not the voice in my head but communication via the TV.

I tried to ignore it. This couldn't be right – the television talking to me! I tried to block it, but the intrusion persisted. Something was happening. The word 'what' was drawing my attention. It seemed as if every sentence spoken contained this word. There were statements such as, 'What did you do?' '*What* time is it coming?' Then: '*WHAT'S* on?' The television appeared to increase in volume each time this particular word was used.

Then the 'energy' arrived; it brought with it a mental compulsion that pushed me on. Even though I was very tired, I dragged my body from the edge of slumber and headed downstairs.

'Where are you off to now?' an exasperated voice called after me from the bedroom. I couldn't reply because I didn't know.

As I walked down the stairs, into my head came the knowledge that I was being given more details for Liz. I made for the study, picked up the telephone listing book and thumbed through the pages, turning rapidly until I stopped at the Ws. My finger ran down the page as if it was being guided. Watson, Watts... At these names it stopped, so I wrote down both. There came the feeling that I must ring Liz and give her one of these names – that was the message. It was too late at night now, but at the very instant that I knew I must do so in the morning, the 'energy' vanished. I returned to bed.

The following morning, I was definitely wobbling. A feeling of having a 'split personality' was washing over me in waves and it required tremendous effort to complete the simplest of tasks. I was walking with a foot in two worlds: one in the physical and the other somewhere in space. Despite being anxious to relay the previous night's message, I was conscious of the need to maintain my balance and therefore forced myself to attend to domestic duties. There was a realization that it was imperative to ground myself by keeping my focus on mundane matters.

Yet the temptation to seek out a closer affinity with this non-physical and mysterious world was strong. I pushed myself along until late morning, when I finally contacted Liz.

We exchanged pleasantries and then I laughingly said, 'Liz, our conversations are becoming increasingly odd, but something else has happened and I know I had to phone you again. I think maybe I've been given the name and address of someone connected with you. I imagine it's something to do with the burglary. It's up to you what you do with the information; my part is purely to pass it on to you. The name is Watson...' Before I could complete the sentence, there was an audible gasp at the other end of the line, then silence. Liz was not a woman normally lost for words. After a moment, I heard her emotion-filled voice.

'I don't think this is anything to do with the break-in,' she said quietly. 'There was a very special man in my life. He died last year. Today I was feeling very upset, because I was with him when he died and this is the first anniversary of his death. His surname was Watson, but I always called him "Whattie".'

This was certainly not a secret I had been privy to. The hairs on the back of my neck stood up and I gave a little shiver. My initiation into this world of magic had so far mostly concerned the realms of the living, but now it was communication from the dead. How could this be?

I had been directed to that name. This was certainly beyond what could be classed as a coincidence. As Carl Jung says, when he writes of how events shift from coincidence to synchronicity, 'Their unthinkability increases until they can no longer be regarded as pure chance but for a lack of a causal explanation have to be thought of as meaningful arrangements.'

The message proffered to Liz had been received with gratitude, for somehow it gave her comfort and alleviated her feeling of loneliness. Belief in the continuance of life in whatever form has been a source of comfort to many bereaved people since time began, and the information that had been sent via me gave credence to this belief. The spin-off also gave me the 'feel good' factor.

The rest of the day I directed towards my family and animals. I deliberately kept myself busy, leaving no time to brood, for my consciousness was still not at its usual level. My senses were heightened and my perceptions uniquely sharp. Everything I touched was sending a hundred sensations through my body. Every color had a multitude of hues; my senses were delivering smells and sounds I'd never before encountered.

In fact the world around me had become a place of awesome beauty. It was as if I had spent my life up to that point in a fogbound enclosure and now the fog had cleared. In the afternoon, as I drove down a suburban road – one that I regularly used – everything was so bright and intense that it was like a paint box picture. The white window frames of the houses were marked against a sky that was an amazing shade of glorious solid blue, and the red postbox stood out like a sentry. All was amazing. It was breathtaking – totally indescribable.

Then the switch went off, and all was back to normal. Unwittingly I had gained entry for a brief period into the spiritual sphere that is the goal of all esoteric and occult adventurers, but as I cleared the evening meal, my senses returned to their previous level of reporting. It felt as if someone had put the lights out. A sense of loss encircled me, a pain of deprivation. Compensation came, however, in the form of thankfulness for the afternoon and optimism that it could happen again: two emotions that were life rafts to cling on to.

So another day on this new and exciting journey came to a close. The night passed uneventfully. The pad by the side of the bed remained unused and I wasn't sure whether to feel relieved or disappointed. I was ignorant of the fact that this was the lull before the storm.

Sunday in our house was my favorite day of the week. It was a casual day without a timetable, giving me the chance to relax and converse with family members who generally called in. In the morning I was mucking out the stables – a task I performed daily – and was quite engrossed in this physical activity when, without warning, the 'energy' arrived. This time it came so quickly and with such a force that I thought my body would explode. I can only compare it with what I would imagine would be a similar sensation: being struck by lightning. A bucket that was in my hand was thrown to one side. My body started to shake, and as I went into spasms of crying, tears started to flow down my face.

There is a reflex in the human body designed to take flight from fearsome situations, and automatically that is what I did. I found myself running across the cobbled courtyard and though the open back door. My mental state had changed in seconds from the calmness associated with mindlessly performing a simple task, to complete panic.

Once inside the house, I started pacing up and down, the energy in my body seeking an outlet. Tears were coursing non-stop down my cheeks. Pictures and words started to flood my head. There was so much that it was on the point of overload.

My daughter, who had been sitting leisurely reading the Sunday papers, rushed to find Barry. But when he approached me I just screamed, 'Don't touch me! Don't touch me! I've got to work this out.'

The scenes in my head were flashing through at a tremendous rate. Words were being thrown at me: sorrow... tears... intrigue... urgency... secrecy... family... With each scene came a change of emotion. The resilience of the human body is amazing; what was happening to my blood pressure at this moment was anyone's guess, but there was a point when I felt I would surely disintegrate.

The moment passed and the pressure eased. All the while, Barry was mouthing soothing words and trying to control and sedate the situation. This performance of mine was beyond the understanding of any of us. The activity in my head gradually cleared, and as it did so, the pacing up and down became less frantic and I finally stood still.

Far from being exhausted, however, my mind was formulating a plan. A sense of purpose was developing.

'I'm going to the police,' I announced.

'No, you're not,' Barry retorted, still in shock. 'Don't be so stupid!'

'I have to! I have to!' I screamed back at him.

He then went into his best counseling mode. 'Well, yes. Okay. Just sit down and work out what you're going to tell them. Write it all down.' He was doing his best to disguise his shock and prevent me from reigniting.

I think at the back of his mind Barry planned to lock the doors and call for medical help. At this stage he was convinced I needed professional treatment from doctors or a psychiatrist. My behavior was totally out of character and I was acting irrationally. Always, when faced with a problem that was beyond his training, Barry would call on the skills of a specialist. My behavior, without doubt, fell into this category.

But I was a woman with a mission; I was aware of what he planned. As I looked around the room, I could clearly read the thoughts of all the members of my family. My brain started to scheme.

'Think I'll go and have a bath,' I acquiesced.

Turning on my heel, I calmly walked upstairs, planning what I was going to do. I started to run the bath and while it was filling I got out some clean clothes. The television had been left on in the bedroom. It was background noise and I wasn't paying attention, when suddenly I snatched up the pen and pad, and wrote,

Irish

teacher

teaches

he is there at the funeral

car

Instantly onto the TV screen came the image of a classroom with children sitting at desks, but that wasn't the whole connection: it was Irish children being taught Gaelic. This scene faded and the first advert of the commercial break started. I don't know what product was being promoted but the scene depicted a psychic driving with her eyes blindfolded and crashing into the back of a police car – an odd advertisement at any time, but auspicious at this moment.

I had my bath and got dressed. All was quiet. Our home had three staircases and I stealthily crept down the back way. I was out of the house and into my car before anyone knew.

Driving along, I did my best to assemble the words and

pictures that had passed through my head. It was like trying to move pieces of a giant jigsaw.

I arrived at the nearest police station and went in, still with no idea what I was going to say. All my life I had been squeaky clean, so coming here felt quite unreal. There remained, however, an unquestioning confidence that I was in the right place doing the right thing.

The desk sergeant politely inquired how he could help. I opened my mouth and a monologue started to pour out.

'Hold on, hold on,' he said, and called for a plainclothes detective who led me into a private interview room. He seated himself at a table, and waving his hand in the direction of a chair, indicated for me to sit down.

For ten seconds I sat there, then once more the powerful force shot through me again and it took a huge effort for me to remain seated. I knew that whatever I was about to report was urgent: the police needed to respond and act quickly and positively to an event that would be taking place in the next few days.

The detective had first requested my name, address and telephone number, and these I had spewed out as rapidly as I could. The important information in my head made it feel like a volcano with the words bursting to get out, so now that the preliminaries were out of the way, the prevailing need was to impart the message. As if on a conveyor belt, the short precise sentences flowed into my head and straight out of my mouth. They poured forth, my normal consciousness contributing nothing to them.

The essence of what I told him was a recap on the burglary at Liz's home, but as I continued talking, it fanned out into much more. The words streamed out of my mouth without seeming to pass through the usual route of my mind.

'There's going to be a funeral,' I stated. 'A very large funeral with a long procession. Many, many flowers – in fact a lorry-load of flowers. The man in the crumpled suit with the dirty white trainers will be there. This man has Eric's American passport. It is imperative you retrieve this passport. But I see him running and there is something to do with a car, but he mustn't get away. It's all so confusing! You must detain him; he's the man you're looking for.'

At this stage I began to get even more agitated. The feeling that this was much more than a normal break-in was overwhelming and I knew the necessity of apprehending this person was of the utmost importance.

Pen in hand, the officer had sat with an impassive face, jotting down notes and continually glancing up at me whilst I spoke. As the speed and volume of my speech started to slow, I got the feeling that as soon as I left the room these same notes would be consigned to a file and allowed to collect dust.

But at that very instant I felt my hair stand on end and a sentence flew out of my mouth that snapped the man to attention. I was so disconnected with what I was saying that I don't even know what was said. But something changed his attitude; I was so in tune with him I could almost read his thoughts. He looked at me intently and started to pay serious attention. I sensed his empathy and felt his need to hear more of what I was saying. He gently started to ask a few questions.

Witnessing the detective's total shift in attitude, I felt somewhat satisfied. Gradually the high-voltage energy and the flow of information ceased, and the part I was playing was complete. As was the pattern, once I had delivered the message, I could revert to being 'the housewife' and resume my familiar occupation.

I drove home. My family members were relieved at my return, but they openly expressed their embarrassment and disbelief at my behavior. That day, I received no empathy or support. They were totally at a loss as to how they should behave, for this was not a situation they had ever encountered.

Somehow I managed to cook the usual Sunday roast but again

I had a feeling of detachment, as if there were a 'me' and an 'I' – a split personality, a self and a shadow self. One part of me was unable to believe I was capable of such extreme behavior, while the 'shadow' half knew that I was doing what I had to do. Thankfully, nothing else strange occurred that day and no further mention of my unreasonableness was made in my presence.

Another day dawned, after a night of no interruptions. I felt normal and able to consider all the events concerning the burglary with a detached outlook. Maybe I had completed my part in the proceedings and it was now past – finished. I reviewed the previous day from the standpoint of an outsider.

The weather was lovely. *Spend some time in the garden today*, I told myself, and that is precisely what I did. It was a glorious afternoon. I trimmed lawns and weeded flower beds, then stretched myself out on a lounger chair to enjoy the warmth of the sun.

I lay there very relaxed. Then I started to feel uncomfortable; there was a tight feeling around my body in my chest, just below the rib cage. Before I could move, it became like an iron band, rapidly getting tighter and tighter. It was restricting my breathing, and a wave of panic washed over me. I was on the point of passing out – everything was going black. It was the same feeling experienced prior to having an operation, as the anesthetic starts to take control and a brief 'zinging' noise is heard before you go under. I felt myself losing consciousness...

Suddenly I 'popped' out of my body. I was above it, looking down and seeing very clearly. Somehow I was hovering above my physical self, able to see my body lying there on the chair, looking like I was asleep. It wasn't frightening and I didn't feel strange; in fact there was a total detachment as I observed the scene. I found it all rather interesting.

Then I started flying, away over fields and hedges. There was no physical sensation, no sound, and no wind blowing through my hair; I was just passing over the very green English countryside at a few hundred feet off the ground, with a bird's-eye view.

I spotted a church in the distance, set on its own. There was a lane to one side, but no houses to be seen. It was small and old and built of grey-colored stone. On two sides were ancient graves, marked by moss-covered tombstones, and to the back was an open field of stubble from a crop that had been recently harvested. I found myself descending towards it, apparently coming in to land. At this point the whole scene grew dim, and then disappeared.

I opened my eyes. I was back in the garden, on the sun lounger, without any trace of pain.

What was that about? I asked myself. It had not been a dream; no way had I just fallen asleep. This experience was not a variation on nighttime dreaming – it was yet another new and unexpected event. How long it took I couldn't tell – anything from two to twenty minutes – and this time there was no presence of the 'voice' or the electromagnetic energy.

I shared this experience with no one. At the time, no one was aware of my inner turmoil; to outward appearances, nothing unusual was showing. I was getting through my days living moment by moment and, because of the Western cultural conditioning we all have, trying to make some logical sense out of it all, for there was nothing I had ever read or heard of that could have prepared me for the trauma of the past ten days.

What I was enduring was a spontaneous and powerful initiation into the realms of the spiritual, and what was to come on the following day would prove to be an even greater test. Recalling it still has the ability to disturb me.

It was 10.00am and the house was empty of the rest of the family. I was to become thankful for that, knowing that they would have been distressed to witness the spectacle of what occurred then. There was just me and the three dogs, who were following me around the house, waiting for the morning walk.

The detailed remembrance of these dramatic events is permanently etched in my memory and my consciousness. I was at the top of the stairs about to descend. Without warning, my legs suddenly turned to jelly as a feeling of utter despair descended on me. Grasping the banister to stop myself from falling, I slumped to the landing floor with my feet on the first step.

One dog sat down beside me as I suddenly experienced such grief it wracked my body. I cried and wailed and rocked my body backwards and forwards. That we lived in a large detached house was fortuitous – there were no neighbors in earshot. Such anguish welled up from deep within me that the only way I could release it into space was by producing animal-like sounds. I hung on to my dog as if she were my lifeline.

For maybe ten minutes I suffered this pain. It was inexplicable and devastating in its intensity. It finally eased, leaving me with gut-heaving sobs and gasps. My body was exhausted. I turned and lay down along the landing, unable to move, my favorite dog stretched out beside me, assuming the role of protector.

It was a while before I could summon the strength to sit up; then cautiously I made my way downstairs. Like a person in shock, I made myself some sweet tea, and after drinking this I felt suitably revived and composed.

At the time, there was no explanation for such an emotional outpouring; I had no idea what had produced it so instantaneously or what dreadful event had triggered such pain. It was later in the day that I started to see the depths of the events that I was embroiled in.

The television news reported the funeral of a British Member of Parliament, Ian Gow, which had been held at 10.00am that morning. This man had been murdered the previous week. The IRA was at the height of their terrorist campaign in England during this period. They had placed a bomb under his car as it sat overnight in the driveway of his home, and as he switched the ignition on in the morning with his wife standing waving him goodbye, the car had exploded, killing him instantly.

The news passed on to something else, but I was left with the story ringing in my ears. It was dawning on me that the horrific events that resulted in this funeral, the break-in and theft of an American passport at Liz's, my trip to the police, and my consummate grief that morning were all spokes of the same wheel. They were all parts of the jigsaw and were starting to come together.

The degree of the range of my behavior was exemplified that evening. On the surface and to all intents and purposes, it was a typical middle-class dinner party, just a small group of friends socializing. The clock said 10.00pm. Was it only twelve hours ago that I had lain exhausted with grief?

One of the guests was talking about a funeral – not referring to the newsworthy item of the MP Ian Gow but to a local service held that day in the same area where Liz lived.

'It was incredible,' I heard him say. 'I've never seen a procession that size for a funeral. The sheer amount of flowers and people was quite unique. There was even a large open-backed lorry to carry the huge amount of wreaths. Apparently these gypsies come from all over the country to attend a compatriot's burial. The police were out in force just to control the traffic. The burial was at that little country church we passed on our way here and the church grounds were like a carpet of flowers.'

There was the other connection. Like a mosaic, the recent paranormal events and mystical insights – these influences from outside forces – all fitted together. Briefly, there flashed before me a three-dimensional moving picture, showing events that were in the process of happening. My facial expression gave nothing away. We all have our secrets, and for the time being, I knew I had to contain mine.

As I was clearing away after our guests had departed, I

switched on the music center. The first words out of the speaker were, 'Just have to say goodbye.' It was the same statement that had been written down in connection to the Marilyn Monroe message – another case of synchronicity.

In the next few days I made a point of visiting the church that had held the funeral service for the member of the gypsy family and it confirmed, as I knew it would, that it was the same grey-stone church that I had visited in my 'out of body' excursion, except that this time I had driven there instead of flying wingless over the fields.

There was also a phone call from the detective who had taken 'my' statement – which had actually originated from a non-human source. He gave his name, then simply said, 'Thank you for your information. I thought you would like to know it was acted upon.'

All of this was just the beginning.

The fear of being overwhelmed by these supernatural experiences was weighted also by the knowledge that our society views all such experiences as aberrations. This knowledge encouraged my secrecy. Our culture regards any extrasensory faculties as suspect, so admitting to the ability to see and hear those who have died would certainly have been deemed hallucinatory and viewed negatively by others. By avoiding entanglement with those in the psychiatric profession, my own innate healing and learning abilities would be allowed, over time, to develop naturally and intuitively.

Had I lived in another part of the world, my experiences would have been judged differently. Amongst certain tribes, an individual with such visible extrasensory perceptions would have been supported. Such a community would have embraced me, and a teacher would have been at hand to encourage these experiences. He or she would have guided me in ways to decipher the visions and would have trained me as a shaman.

Spiritual transformations are historical, cross-cultural

phenomena which can break through in individuals at any time, but each community throughout the world views them from a different perspective. With the arrival of these cosmic forces, my beliefs and philosophy of life, along with my behavior, began to change fundamentally. I commenced a search for understanding – a quest that began with Spiritualism and led me eventually to Shamanism.

Chapter 3

SPIRITUAL HEALINGS

The recent traumatic events had engulfed my days and proved so powerful that all other aspects of my life had, for the time being, paled into insignificance. During the following month, the 'voice' reduced its demands, and the force of the energy that swept in eased; it was then that some order of normality returned to my life.

At this point I recollected several visits I had made to a physiotherapist. These visits had been the precursor to the incredible happenings that were now manifesting around me. What had occurred there had been in milder form, although quite amazing and out of the ordinary. It had taken place prior to these other happenings and had, up until recently, been relegated to the back of my mind. Now, as I regained some clarity in my thoughts and was anxious to understand what had been happening to me, I began to see a connection; this in turn would quickly see me taking my first steps into the area of Spiritualism.

Unknown to me, it was these first few steps that summer that would eventually lead me deeply into the realm of Shamanism. It would be a long while before I would even hear this word and even longer before I gained some comprehension of the world of Shamanism, but in retrospect it is clear that this was the start of my journey and that this period heralded the beginning of a long, arduous apprenticeship and many initiations.

The lives of all of us are involved in an intricate web of links, through a sliding door of circumstance; they are delicately planned and unknowingly we are maneuvered into place. This happens with such split-second timing that one cannot disregard the possibility that there is a pre-planned destiny for each of us. It is only when you spend time retracing an event that you can view the overall plan. From a distant point, it is possible to appreciate how masterful was the arrangement in the placing of those particular events, at those precise times. Over the years, I was to learn that nothing – but nothing – happens 'by chance'.

I now looked back and picked up the first piece of the jigsaw. During a skiing mishap in France that previous winter, my knee had been damaged and I had received treatment from an English physiotherapist staying in the same resort. My minor leg injury required ongoing manipulation, which she recommended I continue after the holiday ended. There is no shortage of good 'physios' in the area where I live, but she said, 'I'd recommend a hands-on practitioner.' So while I waited, she looked through a directory of registered practitioners living in the vicinity of my home and came up with a name. This was someone unknown to her, but her words echoed in my ears as I departed: 'You make sure you go and see her.'

Thus, through a chance encounter, I received excellent treatment from a Finnish woman who was working temporarily in our area. Eila was her name; she spoke perfect English, and although barely five feet tall had strength in her hands unrelated to her small physique: I endured several sessions with her. This woman, with whom I felt at ease, was a diligent worker. My knee injury healed rapidly, causing no further trouble, and there was no reason to expect to see her again. All this had occurred six months previously, back in the winter.

In June, a few weeks before the strange events began to manifest in my life, I returned to see her. I had been having sharp stabbing pains on the point of my right shoulder. The problem was intermittent; some days it was quite acute and on other days it would be fine. There seemed no rhyme or reason for its occurrence.

One day it was particularly bad and my daughter said, 'Go

back and see that woman who sorted your knee out. Phone her now.'

I duly went along for the first of what was a twice-weekly session. This time Eila seemed unable to solve the problem and as the sixth treatment came to a close she said to me, 'This shoulder should be a lot better by now; I can't understand why it hasn't improved. I don't like to continue taking your money. Would you mind if I tried some spiritual healing on it?'

I stood looking at her, nonplussed. Spiritual healing? What was she talking about? I'd never heard of it.

She continued, 'I use this same treatment room; there is no manipulation – I don't even touch you – and there is no charge. I do feel it would help you.'

I felt and looked doubtful, but at that moment I received a sharp twinge in the shoulder. 'Okay, let's try it.' The words were out of my mouth before I could stop them.

I drove home wondering what this treatment was going to be. All it appeared to involve on my part was my time and as there was no fee I figured I had nothing to lose.

The following Tuesday saw me back in the same waiting room. Eila was dressed in her usual white professional overall; her manner was friendly as always. She led the way into the treatment room. In the center of the room was a small wooden stool which she indicated for me to sit on.

She then briefly described her understanding of the term 'spiritual healing'. I listened politely, somewhat bemused, but passed no comment.

'People use various terms for this form of healing, but the source is the same. In effect you do your own healing. I act as a conduit, a battery charger. Around your body is a force field, an aura of electromagnetic energy. It plays an important part in the well-being of the body, but in order to do this it has to be clear and free-flowing. Sometimes a blockage occurs. In simple terms what I do is remove the blockage, thus enabling these energies to recommence their free flow.'

I felt comfortable with the personality of this woman and kept a straight face, but my thoughts were very skeptical of her statements. She continued explaining what she would be doing.

'I work just in this area, keeping my hands about six inches or so away from your body. I won't touch you. You might feel a little warmth or maybe nothing at all. Everyone's reaction is different. I start by standing behind you with my hands above your head; I will gradually walk around you, moving my hands, searching for this blockage. When I find a cold spot I know I have located it.'

There was nothing in that room that was any different from my previous visits – no music, no candles, no incense. The sun was streaming through the window and all was very clinical. Nothing in her manner was any different from on my previous visits and nothing distanced her from her professional occupation.

I sat on the uncushioned stool. She moved behind me and I stared at the plain wall ahead. Out of the corner of my eye I was aware of her hands and I stifled an involuntary giggle.

Within moments a feeling of peace washed over me; there was a sense of comfort, the ultimate security blanket. All muscle tension eased, and my eyelids grew heavy and closed over my eyes. Then it was as if a plug had been removed from somewhere near my feet: there came a feeling of being drained. The sensation grew stronger, as if I was being dragged down, as if the skin on my neck and jaw was being stretched. I felt the corners of my mouth turning downwards.

I thought, *What is happening?* It was impossible to open my eyes – as if my body was moving through a high gravitational force. Then my head lolled to the right and I felt a wonderful sensation: a state of total relaxation. Somehow I remained balanced and unsupported on the stool. Quite what it was that flowed away, I do not know, but at the same time, there was something else coming in. This was entering through the top of my head and the sensation was one of replacement rather than loss. It was a unique feeling and very agreeable.

Next I was aware of Eila quietly moving around me. I tried to open my eyes to see what she was doing but I couldn't – they wouldn't open. I was so relaxed that it was unimportant. I was aware that I was in her treatment room and I heard a telephone ringing in another part of the house. The fact that I couldn't perform this natural action didn't present a problem, as I was floating in a wonderful calm. All the time, I was aware of my surroundings; the knowledge that I was sitting in the treatment room remained and although I retained full consciousness, albeit with a diminishing of my physical abilities, there ran this parallel sense of detachment.

Eila did not talk while she was working and I too said nothing. A gentle touch on the shoulders was the only time her hands made contact with my body and this signaled that the session had come to a close. As if on cue, my eyes opened.

Eila moved around from behind my back and stood in front of me, looking at me.

'How do you feel?' she asked.

'Wonderful!' I replied emphatically.

In spite of the fact that she had stressed there was no fee for this service, because her time and premises had been used I felt obliged to offer her some remuneration. Her response was to tell me there was a charity box in the waiting room, but it was entirely up to me. Her final statement was, 'I hope this has helped your shoulder; I feel it has, but I would like you to come again. I have a feeling that the use of our natural healing energies is the route to clearing this problem.'

I was luxuriating in the sense of well-being and was very happy to take her up on the offer. We agreed a mutually suitable time for the following week.

I left her house feeling elated. This was my first experience of energy healing and I was very impressed. My assumption that this was the normal feeling after such a treatment merely confirms my ignorance of the subject; there was certainly no indication that I was on the brink of a life-changing journey.

This healing, as I later came to understand and appreciate, was the first step in liberating

my natural psychic abilities. Unknown to me at the time, a door to the sacred had been opened, but in retrospect I would see that this had been my first experience of shamanic activity. Eila was the Western equivalent of what is commonplace in tribal cultures. Indigenous shamans know that healing means transformation, not merely the curing of an ailment.

My shoulder improved considerably and I looked forward to returning for another of these healing sessions, even though my family's comments on this unusual form of treatment had been somewhat caustic and dismissive.

I arrived for the second session. The white coat and the neat spotless room that greeted my arrival instilled a sense of security. Again I noted with approval that it was all very professional; I abhorred anything considered 'airy-fairy' or fringe. This time I was determined to keep my eyes open, but within moments of sitting, they involuntarily closed and there was the feeling that a liquid was starting to flow through my body. All was happening as it had the prior time, like a spiritual dialysis with an accompanying feeling of peace.

At some stage I felt a sharp tug on the right-hand side of my skirt and thought, *Who did that?* I wondered if Eila had somehow trodden on it but a few seconds later it happened again and there was no mistaking it. Then there was a flash of a small boy standing by my side. I forced my eyes open. There was no one there and Eila was standing on the other side of me.

The image remained in my head and was very puzzling, but the wonderful feeling of floating removed all disturbances and again I luxuriated in the peaceful cocoon. The gentle touch of her hands on my shoulders indicated that once again the session was finished.

'I thought there was a little boy in the room with us,' I said, looking to Eila for an explanation. She smiled at me but passed no comment.

The tugging of the skirt continued to puzzle me. It was so definite and positive; I hadn't imagined it, but there was no way my skirt had been trodden on, for no part of my clothing was touching the floor. It was a mystery.

I left her house, once again bathed in the glorious feeling of well-being. As I drove home there was a strange feeling that I was looking at everything through a magnifying glass. There was a detail to all that I saw and a sharpness of color. The world looked as if it had been freshly painted: everything seemed bright and new; it was as if I was seeing it all through rose-tinted glasses. I had driven along this road a hundred times but I was noticing many things that my eyes had always missed. It was as if I had been blind and today had been given the gift of sight.

I made a cup of tea and sat on my back doorstep. The kitchen door led on to the high-walled courtyard, south-facing, and today the summer sunshine felt extra good on my face. In this historic house that was now my home I had always had the sense that many others had sat in this self-same spot and I loved to sit here and ponder on who they might have been.

I watched the swallows flying about and marveled at their speed as they continually zoomed into the barn. Then I noticed some ants, equally busy, marching their way around the dogs who were as usual lying at my feet. There was a drinking bowl for them by the side of the step; the water in it sparkled as if it held millions of multifaceted diamonds, and the color in the flowers nearby suddenly took on an intensity and a beauty that I had not been aware of before.

I awakened to an influence from an outside source. I went indoors and checked the answer phone. There was a message from one of my girl friends who was a bit down and asked that I ring back just for a chat. This friend, whose call I promptly returned, had a few years previously suffered what must be one of the most dreadful tragedies that life can impose. Her three-year-old son had been accidentally killed. How can we even imagine the pain a parent endures by constantly carrying this burden? Today she needed nothing more than a listener and thankfully I was able to fulfill that role.

Later in the day I was pondering over our conversation when I suddenly sensed it was linked to my visit to Eila. Until the phone call I was unaware that this was the anniversary of that small child's death. Was there somehow a connection between this anniversary and the earlier feeling of a child pulling at my skirt and the glimpse of the little boy? It was uncanny.

Within days my shoulder was better and it wasn't until my mother asked how it was that I even remembered it had been causing me a problem. My mother had known I was visiting a healer and she too had expressed her doubts, but this rapid recovery impressed her and she exclaimed, 'I wonder if she could do something to help me!' For many years she had suffered chronic back pain. Her search for a cure had encompassed doctors, chiropractors and osteopaths, but none had provided a solution and the only relief was through prescription painkillers.

I called Eila and tentatively requested some of this free healing for my mother, justifying it by explaining that she had tried just about every mainstream option available. Without hesitation Eila told me to bring her along and very generously found time to see her the very next day.

I prepared myself with a book to sit in the waiting room. There was no longer any need for treatment to my shoulder; whatever had been the cause of the pain had been removed. My mother walked towards the treatment room and I remained seated, but Eila, with a nod of her head, indicated for me to follow them in.

She placed a chair against the wall on one side of the room for me to sit on. Mother was seated on the stool in the middle of the room; my position was facing her at about a distance of six feet, which left sufficient space for Eila to move between us. I was pleased to have the opportunity to observe Eila at work with this so-called healing, to be able to watch exactly what she did and to see how she performed the magic that induced the euphoric state. I was delighted to have this ringside seat.

My mother was elderly, on the frail side, and at that time in the first stages of osteoporosis which showed in her posture as a definite rounding of the shoulders. A small wooden stool was not conducive to comfort or a relaxing position. However, without complaint, she sat quietly with her hands in her lap.

Eila repeated to her the few explanatory sentences, in the same words she had used to me. At this point there was nothing hypnotic about her voice nor were her words in any way suggestive. My mother was listening but her eyes were facing forwards looking at me; she lowered her focus to a point around my knees as Eila moved behind her.

I watched closely, understanding as I did the need for such a small stool. Eila was very tiny; her patient's position was related to her needs. First she placed one hand on each of Mother's shoulders, as if lining her up – just a brief and gentle touch. Next she lifted up her arms and held out her hands at a point about six inches above the top of Mother's head. With palms facing down, she held them there for several minutes. She stood with her eyes closed, her face without expression. Then slowly for the next ten to fifteen minutes she moved her hands around the head and torso of the patient's body, slowly walking around her. The palms were kept facing inwards and at no time did they make any physical contact.

All the while, Mother sat still, without talking; her eyes were downcast but they remained open, for I could see her blinking. Once or twice I noticed an expression of discomfort sweep across her face, but that was it. There was nothing else to draw my attention.

Eila concluded her activities by resuming her position behind Mother and once again touching her lightly on both shoulders.

My mother volunteered her side of the experience. 'It felt like something was being pulled out of my back! There was a point when it became quite painful – I nearly asked you to stop.'

I looked at her, saying nothing but wondering why she hadn't mentioned the pleasurable sensations that I knew accompanied these sessions.

Eila made no comment on her statement but simply replied, 'I hope you've been helped', then turning to me said, 'Your turn, Wendy.'

'But there's no need!' I protested. This busy woman was offering more of her valuable time and I found it difficult to accept the gift. But her persuasive words – 'Might as well while you're here' – had Mother and me changing places. Within minutes, the now-familiar 'plug' was pulled and the 'letting go' sensation had commenced.

Halfway through the healing, my eyes sprang open. During the previous session this action appeared to be impossible, yet now, when I was happy to keep my eyes closed, they made this involuntary movement. Something had startled me; there was someone else in the room. I was aware of a presence.

It was the very powerful presence of a non-physical being, for there was no one visible. My senses had communicated this fact and my eyes shot open for confirmation but they reported nothing to my brain. The eyes were overruled; I *knew* there was something or someone there. There was no scent or physical signal, but an overwhelming power definitely filled the room; it was tangible.

As I opened my eyes my gaze went straight to my mother, and the emotion that I experienced was one that today still fills me with awe. Our language is so barren when we search for an expression to convey the depths of the metaphysical. At that moment, as I looked, I felt for her pure *love*. This was a love that is impossible to describe, a love that came instantly, that filled me, and that was beyond anything I had ever physically experienced. What touched me in that room, as we sat in a modern brick-built house in the suburbs of a town in the south of England, surpassed any normal human emotion. It was a sensation I cannot put adequately into words. The love that I felt as I looked at my mother was unbelievable.

There then came not only a sense of wonder and amazement, but also of disbelief and confusion that I should experience something so profound in these settings – and feel such emotions *now*, because like many mothers and daughters our relationship was often fraught and more dutiful than loving. I closed my eyes and tried to hold on to this wondrous emotion, but it slipped away.

It seemed only a few moments later that I felt Eila's hands alight on my shoulders. All I could manage was a weak 'Thank you'. I needed to contain my feelings and thoughts; there was no way I could share this moment. As Mother and Eila conversed I wondered if the power that had pervaded the room had passed them by. They were making arrangements for a further visit, and as I was the chauffeur, they were standing there looking at me for some indication of compliance. All I could do was give an affirmative nod, and mutter, 'That's fine.'

We returned the following week. My mother had not seemed to have gained any relief from her back pain but was accepting once more Eila's offer of help. But after her healing session this time, she was more than a little relieved to move off the hard stool and onto a regular chair. For whatever reason, this didn't seem to be working for her.

When my turn came, I was determined to keep my eyes open; if the unseen presence from last time came into the room again, I didn't want to miss it. I sat on the stool and focused my vision on the figure of my mother. It was to no avail: I seemed to have lost control of my eyes and within moments they had closed. This time it felt as if my head was tipping backwards. There was no drifting into the pleasant peaceful feeling of the previous sessions; this wasn't what had happened before.

Now a picture appeared in my head, almost as if I was watching a screen. A scene unfolded of a straight road. *I don't want to see this*, I thought, and tried to blank it out. *Blank it out!* a part of me demanded. Then an internal voice said, *Think of nothing*. But the scene persisted; it wouldn't change or go away. Simultaneously I was aware that I was in the treatment room and I tried desperately to orient myself to this familiar safe place. But I couldn't. Again I tried to open my eyes, but it was quite impossible.

A sense of panic was rising from deep within me at the sight of this road and once more I tried to find the relaxation that had accompanied the last healing sessions. The same piece of road kept appearing; it was a stretch of motorway that I was familiar with. *Stop it!* I kept saying inwardly. But there was some outside agency that persisted in demanding that I view this road although I didn't want to watch and was fighting hard to block it. For some reason I was becoming very frightened.

Then I saw my car – my very recognizable silver sports car – moving along the road. And I was driving it. The extraordinary thing was that although the picture showed me driving the car, I was at the same time viewing myself from the side. Another 'me' was doing the driving; somehow I was flying alongside it, to the right of the vehicle, about six feet above and slightly behind my seated position in the car, observing it all.

Fear was building inside me; it had all taken on a nightmare-like quality. The car was speeding along the motorway and approaching a slip road to exit it; the fear was growing and closing in on me, and I panicked and started to scream. I had to stop it. I screamed and cried – and everything went black.

I found myself in Eila's treatment room, still sitting on the stool but rocking myself backwards and forwards, unable to stop crying. Slowly the emotions eased and a feeling of relief swept over me.

I was aware of Eila repeating, 'There's nothing to fear. Don't be afraid. There is nothing to fear.' I opened my eyes and gradually calmed down. Mother was staring at me and looking very concerned.

'It's okay, Mother, don't worry,' I managed to say. 'I'm okay now. It's gone. Oh dear, that *was* a bit horrid!'

Eila asked if I wanted to tell what had happened, and as I shared it Mother began to wail. She was convinced that I would be involved in a serious car accident and kept saying, 'What will be, will be.'

'No, it won't, Mother,' I said firmly. 'I feel it was a warning and I won't put myself in that position. When I need to come off the motorway at that junction I shall drive further on to the next one and use the slip road on the opposite side.'

'It doesn't necessarily mean a bad accident – it could just be a minor bump,' Eila added. But I felt she was using those words to comfort my mother. I knew, and I felt she did too, that it was far more than that. The experience left a lasting impression on me and I decided at that moment that I would never use that slip road whilst owning that car.

Before we left that morning, Eila said what I considered at the time to be some very strange things: 'You are needed to do some work and the only way they have of getting your attention is through your emotions. How else can they make contact with you? It is your third eye opening; this is positioned in the middle of your forehead. You may have a pain here for a while – don't worry about it because that is what it is. When this opens you will see things differently. Everything will be clearer and colors will be incredibly vivid.'

At this point I interrupted her to exclaim, 'That's already happening!'

We thanked her, and as we left her home her parting words were, 'Maybe you would like to come to a service at the Spiritualist church? But do call me if you have any more problems.'

The spiritual healing had not eased the pain in Mother's back, and after seeing the state I had got into she chose not to return. Since that time, I myself had no further physical problems so it wasn't until I began my search for an understanding of the extraordinary events of the recent weeks that my thoughts turned once more to Eila.

I was very apprehensive but I made up my mind to pay a visit to the local Spiritualist church, and with this in mind I rang Eila to find out the times of services and also to see if she would be attending the coming Sunday.

She sensed my caution but encouraged me by saying, 'Yes, I'll be there. It's run by very nice people and you'll be welcome to a cup of tea afterwards when you can meet some of them.'

I was happy to discover she was correct, and after several visits she invited me to join with a small group of people who met at her home on a Saturday afternoon for meditation.

Chapter 4

MURDER AND MUSIC

Eila became my mentor. She was the one person I phoned whenever I had a question and always she would be there to pick me up and dust me down. I am sure there were times when she began to fear for my sanity, for this other, non-physical world had invaded my life so powerfully that there were times when it dominated my thoughts and actions, excluding everything else.

She organized a meditation circle which she held every Saturday afternoon. Many months later she admitted that she had started it for my benefit; this woman had felt a responsibility for me, as somehow through the healing session that I had with her she appeared to have awoken a 'sleeping dragon an energetic force contained within the subtle part of the body that I later learned was called *kundalini*35 She described how, during one session when her hands were resting a few inches above the crown of my head, she had felt the sensation that she was touching a large flower bud, and as she moved her fingers she felt this bud open into full flower.

I knew nothing of this at the time. But interestingly, when she later told me about it, I was able to add that the first time in my life that I deliberately sat and meditated, I too 'saw' a large water lily resting above the top of my head, and this flower grew and opened ever wider as I watched. This was in the days before I had ever opened any spiritual book.

I loved these Saturday afternoons. Eila had invited a couple of other women from the church to join us and it was always very peaceful as she led us through a guided meditation that generally lasted about thirty minutes. We would then discuss and try to find some meaning in what we had visualized, have tea and biscuits, then depart. The whole thing took about two hours but I basked in this connection to like-minded people.

I never had a problem following the path that Eila would guide us on as we entered the meditation; the imagery was always clear and colorful, and nothing untoward had ever happened. It was always an enjoyable process.

One Saturday, almost a year after I had first become interested in Spiritualism, I turned up as usual; there was nothing to suggest that today's session would be any different. We settled down, relaxed and closed our eyes, and I followed the path where Eila's voice was leading us. Always it started the same: 'Follow the path up the pink mountain to where the lake is, then sit down and wait and see what happens...' Every week I had no preconceived ideas and was always surprised at what or who turned up!

The lake today was different: it was black and deep, and the land all around was bare. Then on the other side of the water I saw a single tree full of bright yellow blossom – until suddenly a wind swept through and every tiny flower blew off, leaving the branches naked. The blooms settled on the lake where they floated for a brief moment before sinking. The scene was dark and foreboding.

I kept trying to change the image and make the lake shallow and clear; I looked for fishes in it. At one point it did start to lighten and I saw a pink flamingo wading in the shallows, but it was very difficult to maintain and this piece of color soon vanished.

Then into my head came thoughts of a young girl, a student, whom the newspapers had reported missing; she had been gone for several days and it was obvious the police were concerned. I kept trying to clear my mind and dismiss these thoughts, but they continually broke into my meditation and filled my head.

I heard a voice which seemed to be coming from a distance. It was Eila's voice calling us, telling us to come back to the awareness of the room and open our eyes. She held us for several minutes whilst we sat there quietly. No one spoke for several minutes, then she said, 'Return to your meditation.'

I obediently closed my eyes, but as I slipped back into another level of consciousness, I felt everything going black. Immediately, I felt very frightened, then a sharp pain shot across the back of my neck. At the same time, an image of a young girl appeared, standing very close to me, and I could see she was desperately frightened and lost. Simultaneously my head jerked backwards; my teeth began chattering and my eyes made a rapid movement under the still-closed lids.

Away in the distance I could hear Eila's voice repeating the phrase, 'Send her to the light. She must go to the light.'

A beam of light appeared but it was very weak and the girl made no movement towards it. She seemed reluctant to leave me. I felt as if I was physically pushing her and she started to move, but then kept looking backwards and only went halfway there. Yet this was enough to allow me to feel calmer and I managed to open my eyes. I felt more comfortable with my eyes open and after a short while I felt the girl had gone.

I resumed my meditation, returning to the visualization of the lake where everything was now quite beautiful, as I had always previously witnessed it. It had been a very strange and disturbing experience. However, by the time I had had a cup of tea and left my friends for another week, I felt fine and thought that was the end of it. I returned home without giving the experience any further thought.

It was a warm day and the doors were all open. I glanced into the study; my husband was asleep in the chair – an afternoon watching sport on the TV had obviously exhausted him. After the dogs had greeted me, they wandered off and resumed their own activities. I went into the kitchen and sat at the table, idly picking up the newspaper, but before I could start to read it, the familiar feeling of electrical energy surrounded me. My skin started to tingle, my hair 'stood on end', and I began to feel very emotional. Tears rolled down my cheeks as I started to cry and my hands began to shake; I felt that for some inexplicable reason I had suddenly gone into shock.

Then suddenly I was aware of the young girl close to me again. I saw her as clearly as if she was made of skin and bone, although I knew she was not physical. She was about nineteen years old and had shoulder-length fair hair. It was difficult to focus on her appearance as it was her emotional state that held my attention. She was in considerable distress and crying for her mother. She was moving from side to side, clearly anguished and crying hard, calling out, 'Mummy, Mummy!' Then: 'Why doesn't anyone hear me? Why don't you answer?' Again she let out a long wail: 'Where is she? I can't find her. Oh, please help me!'

It was such an extraordinary moment but what made it even more bizarre was that the logical part of my brain came in with the internal comment: *Strange that she's still using the word 'Mummy' – usually by her age it has long been abbreviated to 'Mum'!* For a few moments I was stunned, and then I too became very frightened as her tormented calls of 'Mummy' continued. I felt very shocked. I could see her; I could feel her. What was more, this distraught young person could see me! It was to me she was talking and it was from me she was seeking help.

My tears had ceased. Now my heart was pounding. I knew without being told that this body was caught in an area between two worlds, in a limbo. But what was I to do? As a mother, my physical emotions of sympathy rose to the surface but they were mixed with a fear and bewilderment of my own. Then my reactions became animal-like – and I fled.

I ran to the study and stood in the doorway. My husband still lay there, mouth open, snoring gently. Our relationship was going through a tricky patch, for he was not sympathetic to the unaccountable happenings that had been surrounding me. He was a man with a controlling nature and he found my behavior and talk of supernatural events disturbing. He had no comprehension of what was happening, was very skeptical and found it all highly irritating. He chose to be dismissive – indeed had told me in no uncertain terms to just 'sort myself out' – probably thinking my irrational conduct and actions were related to the menopause and would soon pass if he ignored it all.

I took one look at him, turned on my heel, and went back to the kitchen. This entity was with me – not just following or accompanying me but apparently somehow attached to me. This was another new experience and it was stretching me to the limits. Nowhere in our culture is there an understanding of such occurrences. No wonder so many people with a less strong disposition end up under medication! Our society has moved so far from its roots and lost all understanding of the interaction between the physical and the unseen realms.

This spirit person was still imploring me to help. I sat back down on the chair. It was all quite unreal. The beautiful afternoon was so quiet and still – not the setting I had been led to believe was preferred by ghosts. I tried to block the image of this demanding presence, for although it had invaded my very being, I was no longer frightened. I simply felt helpless; my lack of knowledge made me feel inadequate to the task.

I stood back up, and as I did so, the familiar surroundings of my kitchen seemed to vanish. In its place was another, totally different room where I was standing in the doorway. Once again it was like looking at a large personal TV screen; I was seeing into a room of a typical student bedsit, and although the thin curtains on the bay window to the right of the room were drawn, I somehow knew it was situated downstairs and to the front of the house. The wooden floor had several assorted rugs covering most of it. There was an unmade bed along the wall on the left and I was aware of books and papers and clothes scattered around. Standing in the room were two young people. A male had his back to me; his shoulder-length, straggly hair and casual clothes gave a distinctly unkempt impression. And he was locked in an embrace with the young girl who had been standing in my kitchen moments before.

Then what I saw horrified me, for as I watched he took hold of the scarf around her neck and began to strangle her. As he did so, the sound of Luciano Pavarotti singing *Nessun Dorma* cascaded into my head, sweeping around and around, filling it and pervading every cell of my body. The speed of it all was very strange. I saw the girl die. I saw his adrenaline level drop as the horror of his action began to dawn, but I also saw him lift up floorboards in the room and place her body in the cavity beneath. Then he let himself out of the house and left unseen.

It all happened very quickly, but what I witnessed was in no way 'speeded up', although the whole visual experience must have been very short. Time is such an illusory thing; for each of us, the same hour can pass at a seemingly different rate. All I knew was that I had been watching the 'screen' for only moments while this entire preview unfolded before me.

An awareness dawned on me that this young girl was physically dead but that she was unaware of it. She was lost between this world and the world of spirit. Her image had not faded; she was still standing slightly in front and to my right-hand side, although it felt almost as if she was attached to me. And her cries had not diminished.

I needed help. This was a situation so fraught and so unparalleled, and I was so completely out of my depth, that I had no idea what to do. In desperation I moved across towards the still-open back door, reached for the phone and rang Eila.

The phone had hardly started to ring at her end before I heard her voice answer. Garbled words poured out of my mouth as I tried to describe what I was encountering, but they brought only a calm response from her.

She instantly sized up the situation and I heard her voice directing me: 'Send her to the light.' Then again: 'Visualize a bright light and tell her to go towards it.' She continued, 'Calm yourself down, Wendy, and focus on this light.'

Stillness settled over me at the sound of her familiar voice and I heard myself affirming her instructions.

'Call me later,' she said. 'I'll be here.'

I replaced the phone on the hook and sat down on the back doorstep – that favorite spot of mine. I felt the sun, warm on my face. Everything was surreal; to all intents and purposes this was a regular day, but still this spirit girl remained.

Before I had a chance to concentrate on seeing a light, one of the dogs came trotting from the garden through the courtyard towards me; she had something in her mouth and as she reached me, she dropped it into my lap. It was a baby rabbit. As I picked it up and cupped its warmth in my hands, it took its last breath and died. I felt and saw the spirit of this young animal leave its body, and a transparent 'bubble of energy' started to float upwards and away. As it did so, I saw a beam of brilliant white light start to engulf it. It was nothing to do with the sunshine but a beam that seemed to shoot down from the sky. In a way that is very difficult to describe, it had a spiritual essence – it was a shaft of light like nothing I had ever seen before.

Immediately I felt my inner voice urgently saying, *Go with the bunny! Go with the bunny!* My thoughts focused strongly on this crying girl who remained next to me.

For a brief second all stood still, then there was a movement away from me as the girl loosened her hold, somehow detached herself, and slowly took a step towards the light. Clearly I saw her move into the beam where the energy bubble of the rabbit was already encompassed; the bubble then resumed the shape of the baby rabbit and together they rose upwards. Then the whole scene vanished and I was sitting with a newly deceased baby rabbit on my lap and an adoring dog waiting for thanks for the gift she had brought her mistress.

It was quite a while before I could move. I remained there on the doorstep while the whole episode replayed in my head; it had both mentally and physically exhausted me, and how could I share such an event? My mind was in turmoil. I knew that if I dared to speak of this to my husband, he would be seriously worried. The conditioning of our Western culture would make him view such a scenario as irrational and unacceptable, and he would assume I was on the verge of a mental breakdown. I knew his solution would be to summon a doctor.

Holding the dead but still-warm animal gently in my hands, I went out into the garden and found a suitable place to bury its small body. Then, accompanied by the dogs, I took a long walk through the woods that adjoined our property. The images of what I had seen remained sharp and clear in my mind but it was the sound ringing in my ears that dominated my being, so that I was unable to shift it: the voice of Pavarotti continuously singing *Nessun Dorma*.

That evening, it required a supreme effort on my part to act normally as I prepared a meal for the family and engaged in the general conversation. I made a brief phone call to Eila. Apart from asking me if I felt okay, she pressed no questions on me.

The music was still running though my head but not as predominantly as it had been, and slowly it faded. I slept peacefully that night, and the following day passed uneventfully.

It was on the Monday morning when I opened the newspaper that I audibly gasped. Again there was an article about the missing female student, but this time, accompanying it, there was a large full-face picture. It was this image that had caused my sharp intake of breath, for it was the very same person who had been in my kitchen. The story repeated the facts that she had been missing for several days and her family and the police had been increasingly concerned as there appeared to be no reason for her sudden disappearance.

I battled with what I should do, but later that day I visited our local police station and gave a statement to them. All that I had envisioned on the previous Saturday was shared with them; the officer listening to me asked a few questions but passed no criticism or comments, and I signed a written statement and went on my way. I did not care what they thought of me and knew that whatever my role in this was, it had been completed; it was now all out of my hands.

At one point during that weekend, although I cannot recall the precise moment, another vision had floated in front of me. It passed through very briefly, but its impact registered. The scene was of a beautiful flower-filled meadow, and this same girl, now clad in a diaphanous dress, was skipping joyfully across it whilst alongside her hopped a small rabbit. This picture was mine and I kept it to myself.

It was not until Thursday that the television carried the news that this poor girl's body had been found under the floorboards of her room; the following week, her boyfriend was arrested and charged with her murder. There was never any way of confirming the music that was playing as this horrendous action took place, but it took several years before I could hear Pavarotti's song without once more being visually transported back to that bedsit and becoming instantly troubled emotionally.

It would be some two and a half years later that a piece of the jigsaw connecting to this event would come into place. To further my knowledge, I had booked a five-day residential course designed to help people develop their own mediumship. This was held at the Arthur Findlay College, the home of Spiritualism in England and a long-established institution. The college offers a variety of different courses; there were about twenty students in the group I had signed up with, representing a cross-section of people, but mostly women.

The first two days went well, and on the third morning our task was to stand in front of the group and speak for just a couple of minutes. Each person would be given a different topic but the subject would be unknown until that moment. A single word was written on a card which the teacher would hand to us as we took our place in front of our fellow students.

It came to my turn and the word on my card was 'Forgiveness'. I stood up and immediately confessed that this was one attribute I knew I was lacking; indeed at the time I almost thought of forgiving as a sign of weakness. This was not very spiritual, I know, but that was how I felt and at that point I saw no reason to change my attitude. Barry would often say to the children, 'You know, your mother takes no prisoners!' Vengeance was more in my nature, especially if it came to dealing with those who had in any way harmed my family.

Morning session finished and I sat for lunch with one of the women from this group; she was easy to talk to and I felt an instant rapport. She was about my age, but with an almost unlined face, and she had a serenity about her that added to her beauty; she was one of those persons whom you immediately assume life has dealt kindly with – they must have moved through the years with ease.

As we left the table – she was going to skip class and leave – she said, 'It's such a glorious afternoon! How do you feel about a walk?' I hesitated for a moment, but then agreed.

The college grounds are beautiful, with well-tended lawns, flower beds, and a variety of ancient and magnificent trees. We strolled through them, engaged in general chit-chat, then passed through an iron 'sweetheart gate' where the path meandered and finally led into a churchyard. It was a typical old English church, quite small, and had probably originally been the private chapel to the mansion which was now the college. Moss-covered gravestones surrounded it, with gravel paths running between many overgrown and long-forgotten graves. Here again were more beautiful trees, and apart from us the place was deserted, making it very peaceful.

The door to the old stone church was shut, but there was a bench just outside the porch and my newfound friend suggested we sit down for a while. We sat in silence, enjoying the moment. Then this woman started quietly speaking. Maybe there was something in her voice or perhaps it was some other sense that told me just to listen – to listen without comment or response until she had finished.

Slowly and carefully she began to speak and this is what she said.

'That was a difficult card you were given this morning. To be forgiving is a hard lesson to learn. Just over two years ago, my daughter was murdered. She was nineteen years old, my first child and my only daughter. She was killed in the house where she lived, a place I felt she would be safe, and I had also met the man who murdered her. He was caught and sent to jail very quickly.

'The moment he was convicted, a hatred for him welled up. I hated him so much it is impossible to describe; I didn't know there was that much hate in me. I felt he had destroyed my life, and my every waking moment from then on was filled with his image. My body physically hurt with the loathing for him that I held. Each day began with a rant on how I wished he had never been born and how I desired the opportunity to retaliate and inflict great pain on him. This went on for months and months, the hatred inside me continually burning.

'Then one morning I walked into the kitchen where my husband and son were sitting quietly eating their breakfast. They both looked up at me; they said nothing. They had by this time ceased trying to appease my rants, wearied by efforts that brought no respite to the torrent of my words of hatred. They too had an ongoing task in coping with their own grief at the loss of a much-loved daughter and sister, which they both were handling in a more private way.

'In that moment something happened. I don't know what. There was no bolt of lightning, no voice from the skies. But in that instant I knew I had to change and I knew I had to let go of my hatred. In that instant I knew I had to learn to forgive.

'So very clearly, I saw how my hatred was contaminating the lives of these two people whom I loved the most in the world, and an understanding came that unless I did forgive and let go, I would be guilty of not only destroying the rest of my own life but also ruining the lives of my husband and son.'

She turned and looked at me and smiled, and she looked almost angelic.

Two days later, on the three-hour drive home, I reflected on the course. It had been interesting but not exciting. It was the conversation in the churchyard that dominated my memory. What a story; what an amazing woman!

I pulled up outside my home, but before I could switch off the ignition, the radio – which was tuned to a music station – suddenly seemed to increase in volume as a now-familiar melody began: once more the voice of Pavarotti singing *Nessun Dorma* filled my ears. My whole body tingled as I sat there and listened until the last note faded away. I knew it was one of those beautiful synchronicities, a powerful message. I understood without a moment's doubt that the woman who had so inspired me this past week was also the mother of the young girl whom I had 'witnessed' being murdered.

I like to compare the life we live to that of a tapestry in which each day provides a new stitch. These individual stitches don't make a picture until many more have been added and we take the time to really look at it.

At this same period my husband and I were going through a stressful time because of a situation brought about by my brother-in-law. We had loaned him a large sum of money, as had his parents, none of which had been repaid. I was in the process of pursuing him though the courts on behalf of us both, an exercise that proved exhausting and eventually fruitless. I was furious with him for his behavior and for knowingly placing close members of his family in such a difficult situation.

Although my emotions towards him were not as extreme as hatred, they were not far from it.

I shared with many people the story of the lesson of forgiveness that was delivered in that little churchyard, but never took it to heart as a personal message – some of us are slow learners! It was many years later and not until I had finally learned to let go and forgive my brother-in-law that it occurred to me that maybe all along it was a message for *me*. The universe works its magic in wonderful ways.

Many years further down the line, there once more came a connection to this story. There was a picture and small article in a national newspaper. It was about a man in New Zealand and the wording ran: '… free to live his life in his homeland … this man murdered a young student … now after only ten years he has been released from an English prison'. As I read, I recognized the image and realized that this was the boyfriend whom I had seen in my vision and had described in my statement to the police. This was the man who had triggered such hatred, but who had also been the teacher in the lesson on the value of forgiveness.

Many men guilty of murder, who have completed what some consider relatively short sentences, are released from prisons every year, yet never have I seen a photo and comments about them in the newspaper. Why this particular man? And why at this time? Everything happens for a reason. For me, it was a huge reminder about the need to forgive and maybe a small asterisk in my 'book' to show me how far I had traveled by the time I finally learned this particular lesson. But all that was a long way in the future.

The intensity of these few weeks of 'spiritual emergency' did not last. The constant connection to other realms finally slowed, and the dramatic and often disturbing happenings petered off. To continue at the previous pace would, I think, have put me in a fragile mental state. But the events never stopped completely.

Sometimes there would be a few daily occurrences, followed by maybe a month when nothing unusual happened and my life was very mundane. Then, without warning, something quite unbelievable would occur that would set my mind reeling.

In any case, nothing could ever be the same again. The experience had totally changed my life and put me onto a steep learning curve. My values, my attitude and all of the beliefs that I had held for so many years had been questioned and thrown into disarray.

Chapter 5

SHAPE SHIFTING KEYS

My journey began in earnest as I began to search for an understanding of the events that had occurred. It was clear that much of what I had seen as future events during that period proved over a short time to be accurate; what I foretold became factual.

I became a member of the local Spiritualist church and regularly attended the Sunday services. I read pretty much all the books in the library there and started to put aside a small period each day for myself to meditate. This proved to be a revelation to me, showing me that there was someone or something guiding my life, for shortly after I started doing this – for only about twenty minutes each morning – there came several consecutive days when I was given what I described as 'homework'.

I would sit on a chair and close my eyes, and within moments a name would pop into my head, not of anyone I knew but of some person who had had a little notoriety in the past. Sometimes the name would be in a copy of Debrett's which was in the house, but sometimes it necessitated a trip to the local reference library to read what I could about this person.

To my amazement I found that every single name I was given shared a birthday with a close relative who carried the family name of Taylor.. Maurice Chevalier and Maria Aitken both had the same birthday as my husband, while Chico Marx and Fanny Waterman (an obscure writer I had never heard of) shared my mother-in-law's birthday.

Jack Higgins was another name the spirits gave me; this presented me with difficulties, for it was in the days before computers and access to the Web, so I had to ask my sister-in-law, who worked in the library, to assist me in discovering his date of birth. This she willingly did without asking why, but laughed when she rang back, for it was the very same day as hers!

Then on the tenth day I sat down as usual expecting a repeat of the strange connection as per the previous days, but today no name popped into my head instead there immediately came the phrase 'The time has come.....' I tried to dismiss this and sat meditating for a while longer waiting for a name to appear but nothing more arrived.

As I resumed my daily chores I struggled to make some meaning of it but all I could come up with was the phrase 'The time has come the walrus said' from the poem by Lewis Carroll. It didn't make sense for there was no connection to Taylor but the words stuck in my head and I dutifully recorded it in my diary .

The days of playing this game with the spirits had now ended and it would be many years before I would look back at everything I had written and understand the simple clarity of the message they had been giving me and finally it was so obvious......The time had come. My life was changing beyond belief..

Right now, after the explosive evearnts that had lasted a period of approximately six weeks, my life was settling back into the normal pattern it had run before any of this had occurred. But my mental outlook had changed dramatically; my beliefs and philosophy of life along with my behavior began a fundamental shift. It was only the beginning, but I knew there was so much more to life than I had ever envisaged. The possibilities were endless.

I continued to attend the Spiritualist church, where I found an acceptance of the view that we each have a spirit that continues after the death of the physical body and that it is possible to form a communication with the spirits of those who have departed this life. Eila returned to Finland, but another weekly circle was set up by another member of the church and I was invited to join in with this.

There were periods when I would see auras around people. Sometimes these were composed of brilliant colors like mini-rainbows; at other times there would be minute sparkles like tiny Christmas-tree lights; and once when I was listening to a lecture on ancient Egypt, a bright-blue halo appeared around the presenter's head.

But I was also exposed to the dark side when visions of murders would dominate my day, or spirit beings that had met an untimely death would attach themselves to me. These souls were lost in a 'limbo', unaware that their physical body was deceased. At times like these, I needed to dig deep into my resources of courage and strength to banish my fears and hold myself together.

All of these things I learned to accept, and in return I strove to do my utmost to learn and understand a little of this amazing universe of which we are a part. There was a feeling that I was being schooled; I now see clearly that I had embarked on what was to be a tough apprenticeship.

It was a year later, in June 1991, that I once more experienced several days of extraordinary events. There came an occasion which exposed me to the very darkest side of the unknown, an event whose memory can still make the hairs at the back of my neck stand up. But nothing would stop me from my pursuit of knowledge, and even this experience – which was to be the first of a few in a similar vein – did not detract me from my quest.

In the midst of these almost unbelievable events, I experienced a night that frightened me more than I thought was possible and tested me to my utmost limits. I do not scare easily. Whilst training to achieve my pilot's license, I had faced situations that were quite frightening, times when I had to get myself out of difficulties. When you are 3,000 feet in the air and flying solo in an aircraft, there inevitably come moments when you are severely tested and have to rely on your personal reserves of courage. But the night in question brought me face to face with something totally different: a situation I had never encountered before. It was beyond my imagination and quite terrifying.

There was nothing to warn me of what was to come. Although my every waking moment was still spent walking the 'tightrope' between the worlds – a process which was confusing, difficult, challenging and hard to comprehend – I had somehow been able to handle everything I had been presented with; in fact most of the time, the challenge was exciting. Although I had had moments of apprehension, nothing so far had deeply frightened me. But this was something else.

Barry and I had spent a quiet evening at home and gone to bed as usual; I had fallen asleep without a problem. Then I found myself awake, quite suddenly. I opened my eyes but lay there unmoving. I sensed something in the room; there was no noise, no smell, no disturbance of any kind – but there was something there. It was strong, it was powerful and it was evil.

Our bedroom was very large but I was aware that there was 'something' over in the far right-hand corner. I lay quite still; there was no mistaking what I felt. It wasn't a general feeling of 'something in the air'. This was a huge and malevolent presence, and as I lay there, I was aware of it starting to move; it began to grow. My heart began pounding and at this moment I truly understood the expression 'paralyzed with fear', for every other muscle in my body was instantly immobilized. I was terrified as this 'thing' started to move slowly out of the corner and towards the bed, growing in size as it did. The room was dark and my eyes were closed, but the faculty that I was 'seeing' with was reporting more clearly than any physical sense.

It was then that I entered into a mental battle with this dark force, demanding that it come no further. I insisted that it stop and go back. To start with, it continued its slow journey towards me, still growing in size, and the fear I was experiencing was beyond words. Then, as it reached to within a few feet of the end of the bed, it stopped. Still the inward battle continued. It felt like an eternity as I mentally opposed it, and then there was a subtle shift, a slight diminishing of its size. This moment seemed to give me an added strength, and as I enforced the order to leave, the power seemed to slide out of this unknown thing. It diminished in size and began to retreat, moving back into the same corner of the room where it had emerged.

Then it was gone. The bedroom immediately took on a different energy and all was back to normal. I lay there feeling stunned and it was many minutes before I could regain any movement in my limbs. What happened next came perhaps from my early Catholic training, for the action was performed automatically and without thinking: as my right arm moved across my body, I recognized the first action it was taking was to make the sign of the cross.

Completing that physical symbol was all I could manage. I lay motionless in bed the rest of the night, mentally alert but physically exhausted, trying to make sense of what had happened. There was an understanding that the evil presence would not return, but the first rays of light that signified a new day were creeping into the bedroom before I finally fell back into sleep.

When Barry woke in the morning, I held my counsel and he passed no comment; he had obviously been oblivious to the events of the night. But what surprised me more was that Tara, my constant and faithful dog – the most sensitive of dogs – had as usual spent the night on the mat alongside the bed and there had been not a movement from her during the events of the night. From her resident place she now got up and stretched, and looked at me questioningly. But all she asked was, *Are we going down for breakfast?*

An internal tussle was taking place: should I tell Barry? Immediately I dismissed this thought for I knew it was impossible – there were no words to describe the terrifyingly dark power of that 'thing'. He would certainly dismiss the experience as a nightmare, yet I knew it had been much more than that. Even now in the light of day, when the world usually seems a much safer place, I was still feeling anxious. The sunlight pouring through the windows did little to diminish the recollection of the terror that had engulfed me only a few hours before.

There were no further occurrences of anything similar in my own room, but in other places and at other times I would be exposed to this dark side. It would always come unexpectedly. Each time, fear would strike at my very soul and I would have to reach deep into the well of courage as I passed through it. However, I have survived each episode and have learned to accept and understand the polarity that exists in this life on earth.

It was a couple of months later that this dark encounter happened again, and this time Barry experienced it. We were in Paris for a social event and staying in a grand and luxurious hotel, a favorite place where we had stayed several times before. Earlier that evening we had been guests at a special celebration at which a dear friend of ours had been honored by the French Minister of Culture and awarded the Legion of Honor. It had been a special and very happy occasion; we had a wonderful and fun-filled evening with lots of laughter. As we strolled in a leisurely manner back to our hotel, we were looking forward to a lazy time the following day, with a little shopping and a nice lunch before getting the flight back home later.

It was in this calm and relaxed state that I fell asleep in a grand and comfortable bed. Suddenly I was awake. It was quiet. I opened my eyes but it was very dark and the heavy curtains excluded all outside light from penetrating the room. There was a feeling that I had not been asleep for very long, but I couldn't be sure. I wondered what had awoken me – and then I knew.

Once again on the far side of the room was the thing that had disturbed me. More than black, more than negative, this Evil Thing that I had experienced once before had returned. The voice in my head screamed out, *No! No! No!* as the fear spread through my body. I couldn't see the evil presence. I couldn't smell it. I couldn't hear it. But some extra sense overruled everything and told me there was no doubt it was there.

Only the voice in my head was working, for the terror that came with the thing had again literally paralyzed me. The entity began to slowly grow, but on this second occasion I felt stronger and went into the mental battle immediately. At first it continued to grow and there was a moment when it seemed to be on the brink of moving towards me. This moment is etched on my memory; it seemed to last forever...

But then, just as before, there came an exact point of time when there was a shift of balance. The thing began to diminish, to shrink, fade and then disappear. The energy and atmosphere in the room changed dramatically and reverted to how it had been earlier. I knew it had gone.

This second 'appearance' brought me no nearer to an under-standing of what this entity was and why it should have arrived. This time, it had not had the strength and power of the first occasion, and although it was not an experience I ever wanted repeated, I managed to fall asleep quite quickly. Somehow I felt safe and secure in the knowledge that it would not return that night.

Like most people, I had been exposed to tales of the devil and to pictures of the black-skinned, man-like creature with pointed ears and a spear-shaped tail. I had seen nothing like this emerge from the corner of the room on either occasion, but the terror was such that it seemed to me a demon was most certainly present.

The following morning as I came out of the bathroom, Barry lifted his head from the pillow, looked at me accusingly and said, 'What was that in the night? What were you doing?'

Of course I knew what he was referring to, but in open-eyed innocence I raised my eyebrows and inquired, 'What do you mean?' It was almost a defense reaction, for I was very surprised that he had been aware of anything.

'Something horrible came into the room. Something evil and bad.' He glared at me.

'Well, it's gone now,' I responded, reluctant to even talk about it. Then, with a touch of bravado, I threw in, 'It wasn't as bad as the last time!'

'What *do* you mean? What are you up to? You've got to stop all this messing about!'

It was obvious that the fear my husband had felt was erupting as anger. It stemmed, I knew, from being exposed to events that were beyond his control.

Barry had been taking a 'head in the sand' stance to all the bizarre happenings around me, because he had not yet figured out why or how they were occurring and could not come to terms with this lack of management. Now something had intruded onto his territory – with the added impact that it was very frightening.

Once more I repeated, 'It was nothing I did.'

The subject was closed and he stomped past me into the bathroom. I heard the shower running for a long time; it was as if he felt he needed to physically cleanse himself from the horrors of the night.

Neither of us spoke of this again, but some time afterwards I was talking to a Spiritualist medium who had been sharing her experience of performing a 'house cleansing', ridding it of unwanted energies. I raised the subject with her, seeking an explanation for these two experiences in two different locations. She offered none but suggested that I keep a prayer book in my bedroom with the pages open at Psalm 23, which starts with the words 'The Lord is my Shepherd'.

I passed on this information to Barry; he listened but made no comment. However, the next day I found he had done exactly this. Over the years, wherever we have traveled and in all the numerous different bedrooms we have slept in – sometimes for only one night – he unfailingly makes this his first action.

It was the day following the first incident of what I refer to as the 'Dark Events' that something happened that still amazes me. I feel that the unseen and so-called 'psychic energy' that surrounds us must have been, for some unknown reason, particularly strong that weekend.

For several years I have tried to understand a little of quantum physics, but can get no further than accepting that we are pure energy. However, I hold on to the memory of that particular Sunday morning, June 16th 1991, which proved to me that this is indeed so.

I had been to visit my mother; the car keys were in my hand and we were standing outside her house in the sunshine, chatting as I was preparing to leave. The horrors of the previous night seemed easier to handle as I engaged in this most normal of interactions, though it was hard knowing I could not unburden myself about the Dark Event. I had to accept that it was a memory I would carry alone.

But Mother was a little aware of the mystical events that were happening to me, so I shared with her a tale of synchronicities from the previous Thursday. An invitation to attend a 'Flower Reading' had come from a member of the church. I had no idea what this involved and the lady patiently explained the program for the evening.

'When you leave home to come to the meeting, go into your garden and pick a fresh flower. Cup your hands around it, then make sure you keep it in contact with your own body. This way, your energy will be absorbed by the plant; many personal details will transfer from your aura into the energy field of the flower.

'On arrival you will place the flower on a tray – again making sure, as you put it down, that it remains untouched by the other flowers lying there. When the meeting commences, the medium will be shown the tray holding these flowers and, without knowing who brought which one, she will select one flower at a time. As she holds it, she will proceed to read the vibrations emanating from the bloom, passing back to you the information she receives.

'This information could relate to your emotions, health, the circumstances surrounding you, or anything that is dominant in your life at this moment in time. It's not psychology because she has no awareness of the person she is addressing, and many of the participants she will never have met before. But the accuracy is also very dependent on the ability of the medium. As with every other aspect of life, human frailty means this accuracy varies. However, it's harmless fun and the first steps into a realization of the non-physical world. It offers evidence to prove the existence of auras and unseen energy patterns.'

On my way to this meeting I stopped at a local florist to buy a bouquet as a gift for the hostess. It was midsummer and the shop was stacked with an immense variety of blooms. I dithered for a while, then chose some carnations. They were deep pink in color, edged with red.

The evening turned out to be pleasant, though the readings were superficial. What was memorable were the comments my hostess passed on my arrival, when she graciously accepted the carnations. As I handed them to her, she said, 'My goodness, Wendy! Today is June 13th. My mother was born on June 13th and she also died on June 13th. Her name was Doris and these were her favorite flowers, for they share the same name.'

I was relating this synchronistic story to my mother, and as I was doing so, I became aware of something happening to my car key – it felt unusually warm. I looked down at it and saw that it was softening and losing shape. It felt like warm putty in my hand. I gently pressed the metal and it flattened out and left my fingerprint; then as I watched, it curled and bent downwards over my finger. This took just a few seconds, then instantly the metal cooled and hardened into its new shape. All of this happened very quickly, with my mother bearing witness to the event.

As I stared in disbelief, my mother's only comment was, 'How will you get home?' This gives an insight into the practical, no-nonsense upbringing I had received!

Years later, I discovered that shamans in many cultures, from the high Andes to the lowlands of Brazil, use carnations in their healing ceremonies. This flower has been used from time immemorial and is accepted without question to be a beneficial healing agent. One shaman I later visited used only the petals mixed with oil and rubbed this mixture over the patient's body. Another, when the healing ceremony was complete, took the head of the flower – always a red carnation – and tied string onto the bloom, making it into a necklace which was then hung around the patient's neck. The instructions that accompanied this action were that it was to be worn until all the petals had dropped off.

A third shaman I met claimed that, for healing to be successful, it was sufficient to give him a gift of three carnations before the ritual commenced. When I asked him why the carnation was used, the terse reply was, 'Because it is the most powerful flower', and the look that accompanied this statement implied that surely everyone knew that.

My only experience of healing and the curing of physical ailments, other than by the usual Western medical route, had been via Eila. During the short time I been attending the Spiritualist church, whenever I heard the words 'So-and-so will be available for healing after the service' I had not inquired into this area at all. The other metaphysical events still surrounding me at that time were as much as I could manage, and although the force and multiplicity of them had lessened, I still had no understanding of where they originated and was still spinning from the impact they left. I had neither the energy nor the inclination to start searching into other fields.

Spiritualists are great believers in clairvoyance – the power to see future events and things that exist beyond normal sight. For this reason, my church not only held a regular Sunday service like many other religious denominations, but also provided a demonstration of clairvoyance once a month. Feeling that these meetings might provide some answers, I set out to attend one evening. I was unsure what to expect but was following any lead I could in my desire to learn more about mystical matters.

There were about forty people present; apart from a small group of young people probably in their late teens, the audience was made up mostly of older women. I sat about halfway towards the back and to one side where, as well as having a clear view of the rostrum, I could also observe the attendees. I was anxious to learn, but I was not gullible, and in spite of my personal experiences I questioned everything, took nothing at face value and was looking for clear proof of the existence of other unseen realms.

The clairvoyant who would provide this link between the worlds was a regular, middle-aged man dressed in a suit; nothing in his appearance seemed any different from the hundreds of men who pour out of city offices each day. He was introduced as the medium and started by pointing to one woman sitting in the front row, telling her, 'I am being drawn to you.' Then he began to give a message purporting to come from a long-dead relative of hers. He was quite vague; I had expected names and addresses, but as he moved on, selecting a different member of the audience one by one, it all sounded very much the same.

I watched and listened closely to this man whom we had all come to see, this clairvoyant who offered to present proof that life continues after death, as he told us he was being informed by his spirit guides and that these unseen entities were connecting him with other realms. He claimed to be speaking to an unseen presence, usually a deceased relative of the person to whom his message was delivered. His audience sat in anticipation, each individual hoping upon hope that there would be a personal message, a proof of the continuance of the departed, to comfort them in their grief or loneliness..

I was not impressed. It was all very vague and 'wishy-washy'. I expected him to be delivering information as specific as that which had peppered my days, but this was not happening. After he had spoken to about five people, I felt myself looking at him in disappointment, and then anger started to rise accusingly. I felt he was a charlatan, massaging his ego, for there was no empathy in him. At that point, he was giving some uncalled-for advice to a member of the congregation and was disparaging in his comments about someone he claimed was a neighbor of theirs.

I felt my anger start to increase; tolerance was a quality which I was lacking at that time. I glared in his direction and was on the point of leaving when something rooted me to the spot. Without warning, an apparition appeared around him. My anger turned to awe as a halo suddenly formed.

At first it was just around his head, in the shape of a thick, white, creamy band that extended about twelve to eighteen inches outwards. Then it grew and extended over his shoulders and partly down his body. It didn't obscure any part of him; it extended out from him and was so thick that it appeared solid, for it was not possible to see through it. It lasted for several minutes, leaving me dumbstruck, as the experience was totally unexpected and evidence of yet another phenomenon I had never heard of.

I closed my eyes and then reopened them; I looked away from it and then back; several times I repeated these actions, but still it was there. The medium was seemingly oblivious to this phenomenon, as were the other occupants of the hall; no one gasped or made any comment; no one was staring at him with their mouth open, as I'm sure I was.

The vision of this aura lasted for a while as he continued talking; then, without any visible change in his attitude, it vanished. My desire to leave had gone and I remained seated, willing the halo to return, but there was no further sign of it. The speaker's attempt to pass on messages from the dead were in my opinion feeble, but I was a newcomer to all this – what did I know? The rest of the attendees seemed very accepting and were hanging on his every word.

In spite of my disappointment with the quality of the offered clairvoyant messages, my head was filled with the image I had seen, and before the session finished another odd thing happened. My hands, which were resting in my lap, started to tingle; then came the feeling of 'pins and needles' going through my fingertips and running down the outside of my thumbs. I started to notice my hands getting very hot; the rest of my body felt comfortable and was not changing temperature, but something was happening to the palms of my hands. I opened them out and glanced down at them: it felt as if each hand had a red-hot core in the center, but there was no visible sign. This phenomenon was an added unexpected occurrence, again beyond my expectation, and it left me feeling very bemused. The heat in my hands faded after a while and I left the hall that evening with more questions than answers.

Over the next few days, this sensation would unexpectedly recur, although there seemed no rhyme or reason to it. I resorted to the medical books but could find no explanation and once more had the sense that it was connected to my spiritual learning, especially as it had started in the middle of a church service. It almost seemed as if witnessing the 'halo' had triggered it.

Again it was to Eila I turned for an explanation. After I described the symptoms to her, in her brief no-nonsense way she said, 'It's healing heat.' And in response to my question 'What do I do about it?' she said, 'Use it!' That was it!

So I made my first foray into 'spiritual healing'. It was a great lesson in learning to listen to my intuition – a word whose literal meaning is simply 'inside teacher' – and my first patient was one of my dogs who was unwell. I started by copying Eila: holding my hands about an inch away from my pet's body, I moved them across her side as she lay stretched out on the floor. Very quickly the dog seemed to relax, her breathing became less labored and she drifted off to sleep. I sincerely felt it had helped.

A few months passed and my life settled back into the usual domestic routine. I continued to try out the new healing technique, which definitely seemed comforting to my animals and was also successful in curing a friend's hangover; in addition I practiced on my mother as it seemed to help with her back problem. I was putting aside half an hour each morning to sit and meditate, and was still a regular attendee at the Spiritualist church, but that was all. I wanted more. My desire to find the meaning of the extreme experiences that had interrupted my life remained, but I didn't know where to extend this search.

My husband and children were happy that the center of the family was back in her familiar role. The six-week span of strange behavior on my part had disrupted the calm of our household and frightened them, and although they were unwilling to discuss that episode, they passed no comment on the change in my reading material and quietly accepted my need to attend the 'fringe denomination' service every Sunday evening.

Then, once more, there came an unexpected event. It was as if the gods had parted the veil and gifted me with another glimpse of the 'other side' to encourage me.

With a small group of friends, I set off on what had become a regular once-a-year skiing holiday. One of the members was Pauline, the physiotherapist who had moved to the north of England the previous year and had referred me to Eila.

So much had happened in a year. Pauline is an empathetic and caring woman, and I knew she would not dismiss or disbelieve anything I told her. I knew she would be interested, listen, take it on board and make her own decisions as to whether I was delusional or whether there was truth in what was being said. We were room sharing and I couldn't wait to share with her what had happened as a result of her producing Eila's name. It was one of the many instances when I could see the miracle of the Oneness of our lives – how we are all connected as if in a great cobweb.

Pauline is one of Nature's carers. Her training and skills as a physiotherapist lead her to focus on healing, and it was she who brought up the question, 'I wonder if this form of healing will work on Jill?' She was referring to a mutual friend of ours, a member of our skiing party, who had for many years tried to get pregnant; this woman so wanted to have a baby but had recently been told there was very little hope of it happening.

Jill was open-minded and ready to try anything, so one evening the three of us gathered together. As we were preparing to find a quiet space, a friend of Pauline named Ian, who had accompanied her on this holiday, asked if he could join us to watch. The rest of us had met Ian for the first time only a couple of days previously; he was a quiet and gently spoken young man in his mid-twenties, just embarking on a career in nursing.

We moved off into the room that Pauline and I were sharing, taking a stool from the chalet's main room with us. The bedroom was quite spacious with a small settee on which Pauline and Ian sat to observe.

Jill seated herself on the stool, leaving me enough space to walk around her. And so we began. My hands were tingling as I held them close to her, and for a while I held them steady over her head and stood with my eyes closed. Immediately, in my mind's eye, I saw a white-layered crib with a tiny baby in it. I saw Jill and her husband Pete standing by the side of this crib, gazing with wonder into it; the baby had a mop of dark hair and appeared to be only a few weeks old. The image was clear and detailed.

The connection and the energy I felt was very strong and I continued to hold my hands close to Jill for about fifteen minutes. Then, as in the sessions I had enjoyed with Eila, the 'plug' was pulled: the sensation I had felt – as if a cloak had been placed around me – began to lift and then was gone.

I touched Jill lightly on the shoulders. She looked at me and said, 'Is that it? I didn't feel a thing!'

I shrugged my shoulders, not sure how to respond. 'Perhaps you weren't supposed to,' I offered, and bit my tongue to prevent saying anything more, because I already knew better than to share my vision.

It was then I heard Pauline say, 'Looks like Ian has fallen asleep!' I turned my head and looked in his direction. Ian was sitting perfectly still; he was upright and unmoving, but his posture belied her comment. As the three of us stared silently at him, he opened his eyes wide, and through clenched teeth said, 'I can't move!' We stared at him, thinking at first he was joking, but he wasn't. It was as if his body was frozen, for he was totally immobile. His hands were resting in his lap with the palms facing upwards, his feet were square on the floor and his back held straight and rigid. It was as if he was in a catatonic trance.

I quickly moved in front of him and somehow talked him back into mobility... but it was a scary moment, both for him and me. He claimed that nothing like it had ever happened to him before. He had felt perfectly fine until the healing started, and had no explanation for what had happened; he was looking to me for an answer, but I had none.

Several very strange things happened later that were connected to this evening. The first occurred on my return to England. On the morning after I had arrived back, Barry and I were sitting at the kitchen table. 'Well, tell me about your trip,' he said. And I made the mistake of telling him about the healing session.

Barry was utterly dismissive and made a sneeringly caustic remark. It was as if a fire shot up through me. I knew that what had happened in that skiing chalet had been very powerful; I knew it and I felt it, and now I was extremely angry that he could talk disparagingly about something that was undoubtedly sacred and precious. Jumping up, I grabbed my car keys from the table and swept out of the door, not sure where I was going but feeling a need to escape and distance myself from such scathing words.

As I approached my car, I felt heat in my hands and the keys 'wriggled'. At the car door I looked down at them; to my utter amazement, I found the metal had turned into a tight spiral and had solidified in that shape. This sounds unbelievable, but it happened!

The second occurrence came several months later, when Ian shared with Pauline the news that he had just completed treatment for testicular cancer – a condition he had shared with no one – and had now, happily, been given a good prognosis. I wondered if the healing energies that were present that day in the French Alps had somehow been redirected to Ian.

The third event was that Jill and Pete many years later adopted a six-year-old boy; it was a while before I connected up the dates, but he was in fact just one month old when we were on that auspicious holiday and I saw the vision of the dark-haired baby. Their son has Maltese natural parentage and jet-black hair. Life takes many twists and turns, and it is never as we think it will be.

Chapter 6

GUIDANCE FROM AN ANCESTOR

My life on the outside appeared quite 'normal', and apart from a drastic change in my reading matter – I never read a novel or any fiction again! – it continued much as it had before the advent of my 'spiritual emergency'.

I continued to attend the Spiritualist church, but the attraction was starting to pall. Occasionally there would be a visit from a medium who would produce convincing proof that life continues in spirit after it leaves the physical body, but this was the exception; the majority of the claimed connections that emanated from the rostrum were vague and gave nothing specific. The problem was that I was unsure where to look next, but every so often something would happen to hold my focus and energize my ongoing search.

There had never been what I felt was any direct contact with my own ancestors. I had neither seen nor had messages from my father to whom I had been very close and who had died when I was only twenty-two. Neither had my maternal grandmother – a beautiful Irish woman who was long-deceased – made an appearance. As a child I had been enthralled by her stories of pixies and fairies, and I never doubted her when she assured me that Ireland was full of the 'wee folk'.

But although I was unaware of the presence of my ancestors, there came a day when I was given a sign that they were still near, closely watching over not only me but also extended family members. Occasionally synchronicities are so orchestrated that they move beyond the order of chance; I believe in this case they are engineered by our angels or guides. When this happens we are aware that, like pieces on a chessboard, we are being moved into place. This was one of those events.

That day, I was commencing the usual housework routine when the desire to telephone one of my aunts entered my head; this woman, who had married my mother's one and only brother, had endured a life marred by tragedy. The urge to phone her became very strong; at first I dismissed it, for there was no reason to do so. It puzzled me why I should want to – I couldn't remember ever having called her before – but the idea remained and grew ever stronger. Finally I dropped what I was doing and dialed her number... There was no reply, which was actually a bit of a relief for I had no idea what I was going to say when she answered.

Betty lived only a few miles away, but I saw her rarely and kept up to date with her health and well-being through other members of the family. My mother was one of six sisters, and this aunt who had married the only boy in the family was considered the seventh sister. As a child, I had stayed with her on many occasions, as her two daughters were quite close to me in age. Sadly she was now a widow and both of my cousins had also died, one in her early thirties and the other just over a year ago. Although my aunt lived alone, she was fit and active and kept busy. We would meet at family weddings and funerals, but apart from a few lines at the bottom of the Christmas card, we had had no direct communication for a long while.

Despite receiving no reply to my phone call, I was drawn to try a couple of more times. But when I still had no success, I pushed this inclination behind me.

Later that day, I was in our village shop buying a few groceries with nothing more important on my mind than planning the evening meal, when the 'plugged in' feeling swept over me. This time it took total charge of my physical body; there was no way I could argue or divert my actions. Without a moment's hesitation I dropped the basket of groceries to the floor and fled from the shop, jumped into my car and sped off.

It is very difficult to describe these non-ordinary experiences. Our language has evolved and lost the words to cover occurrences of a mystical nature. The existence of a supernatural force has for the most part been denied, and indeed in England, until the repeal of the Witchcraft Act as late as 1949, dealings with this other reality were deemed punishable by imprisonment. How do you explain how a housewife, living in the English suburbs, was consumed by a power that was invading her thoughts and directing her actions – a force that arrived instantaneously and was impossible to ignore? I felt like an automaton.

As I headed off, I knew exactly where I was going. The force in my head was directing me and I knew I was on my way to a cemetery several miles away. There was no rhyme or reason to do this and at this point I had no idea *why* I was going there; all I knew was that I just had to and that it was urgent.

A red-light indicator on the dashboard of my car flashed on, a warning that the fuel level was low. I ignored it, continuing past several garages. This was totally out of character, for to risk the inconvenience of running out of petrol was a situation I would definitely normally have avoided. However, I did not stop; the force directing me overruled all normal rationality.

Many years ago, I had had a friend who lived about fifty yards from the entrance of my intended destination, but that was the closest I had ever been. The traffic was light and it took me just over ten minutes to get there; I pulled up outside the large iron gates, parked at the curbside and got out of my car.

Before I could even question why I was here, the answer came immediately – for as I turned towards the gates, the aunt I had been continually phoning walked out! We stood there face to face. Her amazement was as apparent as mine.

'What are you doing here, Wendy?' she exclaimed.

'I honestly have no idea, Auntie Bet.' This was the only response I could give. But I did add, 'I have a feeling I've been sent here to see you.'

She asked no more questions and was just happy to see me, seeming somehow comforted by my presence. We stood there in the early spring sunshine and she told me she had been tending her family's graves, and invited me to go back in with her and visit them. So I accompanied her back through the high iron gates. Walking together arm-in-arm, she guided me to her family's graves and I looked down on the place where my uncle and both of my cousins were buried. As we stood there listening to bird song, I offered up a silent prayer.

'I'll drive you home,' I said. 'It'll save you catching the bus.'

'Thank you,' my aunt replied, then added, 'Are you in a hurry?'

'Not at all,' I answered as we strolled along.

'Well,' she went on, 'your grandmother is buried here. Did you know?'

I replied in the negative and had to admit that I'd never been in this place before and had no idea that this was the old family cemetery nor where my grandmother's grave was.

This cemetery was vast; it must have been the original burial ground for the town, for there were acres of graves. Aunt Betty proceeded to lead me through a maze of paths between ancient headstones to a far corner, before she stopped and said, 'It's around here somewhere.'

We started to read the names on the stone markers and after a few minutes she found it. I moved to her side and saw the etched name of my maternal grandmother. As I read for the first time the inscription on my ancestor's tombstone, I recognized her name, but it was the date that transfixed my gaze and made my hair stand on end. The date of her death was March 1st, a fact I had been unaware of, but I did know that this day happened also to be March 1st; it was the thirty-second anniversary of her transition.

Suddenly I understood that this was all her work. From some unseen place she had been watching this woman whom she considered a daughter, as she suffered anew with the pain that comes when loved ones depart from this lifetime prematurely; my grandmother had been watching as tears were shed, and had been moved to try and ease Betty's pain. I was used as a messenger and had been sent to provide my aunt with company.

We both remarked on the synchronicity of the date, and as I drove her home, discussing our mutual belief that life does indeed continue after physical death, she shared this story with me.

Shortly before her second daughter died, Aunt Betty was convinced that her long-dead husband had appeared to her. She had been alone in the house one afternoon, sitting in the armchair watching television, when she became aware of someone standing beside her. As she turned her head, she had a glimpse of her husband standing in the room, smiling at her; the vision was very brief, lasting only a second, and she could not understand why it had happened but had no doubt that it had.

Her daughter died suddenly two days later, and many weeks passed before it dawned on Betty that he had come to collect her and guide her to the other side. She had always hung on to this belief that her husband had returned to escort his daughter to what one beautiful hymn calls 'the Summerland'. The glimpse of him, and the timing and place, convinced her she was right, and she said the memory of this vision had given her a lot of comfort.

Who can doubt the pain my aunt endures as she tends the graves of her whole family? Somehow, on that particular day, a response was forthcoming from another dimension to retrieve her from the pit of despair and isolation. My belief is that my grandmother, still loving her only son's widow, guided me there that day. In doing so, she provided comfort, strengthened my aunt's belief that life does indeed continue, and opened the doorway to her connection with me.

Slowly over the next two to three years, I began doing some platform work for the church – not clairvoyance but leading the part of the service that is referred to as 'the address'. Here I would share with the congregation some of the events from my life as, for me, these gave overwhelming evidence of the existence of other dimensions. I was also chairing a weekly discussion group where the subjects covered healing, reincarnation, spirit communication and metaphysics in general. My knowledge of these subjects had come partly from my personal experience but mostly from a sponge-like reading of any material I could get my hands on and also from listening and dissecting any talk on the paranormal.

My search took me from 'psychic fairs' and tarot cards, into numerology and the exploration of I Ching. I researched the Gnostics, browsed through the Kabbala, read books on Buddhist beliefs and touched on other religions and dogmas. It was a continual and ongoing search, for there was an ever-growing awareness deep within me that our material lives and constant focus on consumerism were a mere cover for the true meaning of our existence.

I made my own judgment, being open to all I heard but then intuitively filtering it. All information I would either accept or store, waiting for further development before I considered either taking it on board or discarding it. There was never a repetition of the original awesome six weeks, but mathematically and highly impossible coincidences continued to pepper my life.

Each morning for half an hour I would meditate, but there was also a further regular evening set aside for what was called a 'circle': a period of group meditation. Each week on the same day and at the same time, our group would meet. It was at one such meeting that there was an incident that was to test me to my limits.

There were five of us who came together; we were like-minded people and comfortable in each other's company. We had been meeting for over two years, only missing an evening if we were ill or away on holiday, and a bond had formed between us;

we trusted and respected each other.

My companions had been long-time members of the Spiritualist Church and all held the firm belief that the spirit is eternal: when at death the physical body is discarded, the essence of the person continues, albeit in a different realm, and there continues the possibility of communication. This belief shared by these caring, responsible members of our community was a great comfort to me. When I was first aware that the unsolicited messages I had been bombarded with were communications from a non-earthly realm, these were the people who assured me I was not losing my sanity. My friends were sensible, down-to-earth people, not given to fantasy. We were all of a similar age and outlook; we believed in personal responsibility and were certainly not of a gullible disposition.

Mike was the lone male in our group; he had held a senior position in the police force before taking early retirement. Now he was running a house-letting business; Angie, his wife, helped run the office while he engaged in the practical side, repairing and restoring properties after bad tenants had departed. His job exposed him to some of the less attractive sides of human nature, but he was always calm and his wicked sense of humor would often have me collapsing into giggles at one of his irreverent remarks.

Of the other three women, Anne was the quietest of us; she worked full time as a health care visitor and always said how she enjoyed the peace of these Friday evenings. For her, they provided a little break from her home where her husband and two strapping sons dominated the sports-focused conversation.

Lucy was the original 'Earth Mother': very tactile, she greeted all she met by enveloping them in a big hug. Her days were still filled with looking after her large family, for she minded grand-children while their parents worked full time, and she was always the first person to answer the call of any neighbor in need.

The final member of our circle was Margaret, a woman with astonishing energy. She was the archetypal symbol of the saying 'If you want something done, give it to the busiest person you know'. Not only was she a midwife, but she was also responsible for the local doctor's mother-and-baby clinic, ran the area meeting of the Girl Guides, visited the housebound and was president of our church. These were just the tasks we knew about; in the case of such a special soul, numerous kind gestures would have passed unrecorded.

They were all loving people, grounded in their daily activities, and they were my anchor as I continually walked the tightrope, balanced between the two worlds. These were the only people who understood a little of how arduous my days would often be. With their help and support, I was learning to accept the unexplainable and the unproven.

Our evenings together followed the same pattern: we met at Lucy's home, a house in a quiet residential suburb of Southampton, similar to thousands all over the country. Prior to leaving home, I would almost ritually prepare myself as I refrained from eating for several hours and bathed in scented waters. This was instinctive behavior, as deep within me there was the knowledge that I was entering the sacred – barely touching the perimeter but nevertheless intending to contact these other worlds. I was seeking guidance and wisdom from the ancestors and the spirits, and I felt a deep-rooted sense that this deserved preparation and a full degree of respect; there was a need to enter this circle both physically and mentally prepared.

My knowledge of the other worlds was still meager, but because of the particular incident with my aunt, there was a belief that the spirit of my maternal grandmother was often lurking nearby.

For our regular Friday evening group meditation, we would arrive at approximately 7.45pm. Lucy would greet us and lead us quietly into her sitting room. A large candle would be alight in its holder on the coffee table, and a small lamp on the side provided subdued lighting. We sat in an arranged circle on comfortable chairs; there was no talking at the beginning of the evening and all general conversation was withheld until the purpose of our meeting was fulfilled.

Once we had all arrived, our hostess would signal the beginning by offering a few words of prayer and a statement of intent, namely that we were gathered in the search for spiritual wisdom, seeking knowledge and help from our ancestors for ourselves and the community. We were reaching out to the unseen spirits, offering ourselves as a channel for communication between the worlds. This modern-day setting was in effect no different from those of indigenous tribes, living in remote mountains and jungles, whose members still gather to call on the spirits for aid in their daily lives.

An audiotape recorder was set on the table, switched on and left running. Then for one hour we would sit in meditation. Religion has its origins in altered states of consciousness; it has been proved that when we focus attention just on our breathing, the beta waves of our brains change their pattern. Always my aim during these circles was to simply quiet my mind – to open it and allow it to be the transmitter for information from elsewhere; it was all very naive and unstructured.

The silence would be broken only occasionally by one of us wishing to share information that we were receiving. Sometimes this would be to describe the essence of a person that we felt was drawing close. On occasion it would be a positive revelation and many times two of us would be tuned in to exactly the same thing. Carl Jung referred to the 'universal consciousness', and modern physics is beginning to accept the possibility of parallel worlds and energy dimensions.

There was an instance one evening when I felt myself transported to a different planet where I interacted with non-human entities, my mind all the while trying to reject what it was seeing.

This episode I kept to myself; I had learned to bear the isolation that resulted from the inability to share some visions. There was still a fear of ridicule and social ostracism but also a deep-rooted instinct that this was not what my companions were seeking and was beyond their comprehension.

The success of my search for an understanding of the metaphysical events that continued in my life had to this point been limited. I had still neither met anyone who had had the same wide range of personal experiences nor read any modern records of such a person. The phenomena were still happening to me, but now I was grateful for them and accepted them as gifts.

This particular Friday evening was, on the surface, the same as every other, and my day had offered no hint of the bizarre event about to unfold. I had prepared for the evening as I usually did; always I obeyed the urge to separate the day's normal activities from the spiritual event of the evening. My instincts had always led me to treat these activities with awe and reverence.

All five of us were present this evening. I entered into the meditation no differently from a hundred other times, allowing thoughts and images to present themselves, then flow onwards. There was no sound from my companions, just the occasional crackle from the burning log fire. Then at some point, I became very conscious of my physical body, of my arms in particular. There was an awareness that they seemed to be shrinking. There was no mistake about this – and it was the most bizarre sensation. It was not that I had lost feeling in them and was devoid of a sense of my arms. Not at all; rather, it was a definite sense of them retracting, sliding back into my shoulders. Then I felt my body elongate, as if I was being pulled upwards; my neck grew in length.

My consciousness separated into two parts. There was one part that comprehended these sensations and flowed with them, secure in the understanding that it was natural and there was nothing to fear. The other half was demanding to know what was happening but simultaneously aware that it had no control and that its role was that of a passive observer. As my mind was absorbing these sensations, the energy of a snake enveloped me; I felt like a snake – that I was a snake. I felt my body start to weave and sway, and then came clarity: I *knew* I had become a snake. No longer were there questions. I *was* a snake.

I felt myself coil backwards ready to strike; there was anger in this entity. The essence of Wendy had moved to one side, and in her place was a disturbed and angry snake. It lunged and spat. At first, it focused its venom at Lucy who was sitting to my right, and then it turned and hissed and spat at the rest of the group. For several minutes, as this energy held prominence, these actions continued and there was no comprehension of where it had come from, why it had suddenly arrived, or why it was so angry. It just was, and this fact was translated by its sound and actions.

Then slowly the hissing ceased; I felt myself coil downwards. As the snake energy subsided, there was a sense of draining, of something leaving my physical body before the awareness of my human body and its normality returned. I sat there quietly, my restored rational mind thinking, *What on earth was that?*

There was no fear, just wonderment. Although I felt physically tired, in my head there was an 'acceptance', which seemed a strange description. I was very puzzled, but immediately, through a deep-rooted wisdom that lay in my heart, I knew something very special had happened. How could I comprehend such an incident? Nothing I had ever read or heard gave me even the smallest clue.

Lucy brought the meditation to a close with a prayer and we sat there in stunned silence.

I slowly opened my eyes. The faces of my friends betrayed their emotions; each showed something different: fear, excitement, concern and incredulity, all laced with a smattering of shock. Due to their caring natures, they first enquired how I was feeling and then looked to me for an explanation, but I could offer none. They were in total agreement that they had all witnessed a snake.

Mike was the first to share his view from his seat beside me. 'Are you all right, Wendy? What on earth happened? I heard you making these noises, but when I looked I *saw* a snake. It's difficult to believe but I know that's what I saw.' He got quite animated and continued, 'It was so real I moved out of the way when you came in my direction!'

Lucy jumped in with, 'It was incredible. Your face changed shape and your skin became sort of... Well, I know I saw scales.'

As the others voiced their comments, I listened, volunteering just a little. Margaret and Anne both expressed what they had seen. Amongst all four friends there was total agreement that it was the manifestation of a snake and indeed three of the four claimed to have witnessed my skin take on a scaly appearance. But Anne was visibly shaken and admitted to closing her eyes after the first glance.

'I really was frightened,' she said. 'I don't want any more of this.'

Margaret seemed concerned that my behavior was somehow detrimental: 'I've been in the Spiritualist movement for many years and I've never heard of anything like this happening. I feel rather concerned about it.'

I sensed that she felt an unwelcome dark element had invaded the circle.

Once again, Lucy voiced her opinion. 'I know what I saw,' she emphasized.

But there was a general reluctance to disagree with the opinion of Margaret, who was a long-time friend. Like all creatures, human beings have a fear of the unknown. The overall consensus was one of awe and bewilderment – none of us had even heard or read of the evening's phenomena. Only Mike remained excited, male testosterone overruling the spiritual aspect. None of my friends had any idea of what had happened; they were bewildered and devoid of any explanation.

A reminder of the evening's events was provided by the audiotape that had been set on the table; it had recorded both the hissing and the comments. Later, when I listened to it, the sound was reminiscent of a large snake disturbed from slumber. I made sure to record the incident in my journal, but without explanation, for I had none. It would be three more years before the term 'shape-shifting' would enter my vocabulary and give me a clue towards an understanding of that evening's events.

I left the meeting soon afterwards, feeling a need to be alone. My four companions remained; I knew they also needed space to discuss what had occurred without being inhibited by my presence.

As I drove home I had a sense of awe. From deep within my core came the knowledge that we had been privy to something extraordinary, something beautiful and sacred. The roads were quiet and my car was soon crunching down our long gravel driveway. There were still lights on downstairs, but there remained a need to be by myself.

Turning away from the house, I walked towards the stables. At the familiar sound of my footsteps, a white horse's head appeared over the half door and a gentle whicker greeted me. I opened the door and stepped in; then, burying my face in the neck of my beloved horse, I began to sob. He stood still, the energies flowing between us, and I felt he understood the gamut of emotions I was feeling. We were connecting in a way that I had found impossible with humans.

That evening was to be the last group meditation I attended. Although, as individuals, these were kind and generous people, the incident had triggered a fear – a fear born of ignorance that is always magnified when held within a group. In the following days, Margaret consulted with a person who held a position of authority in the echelons of the Southern Area Spiritualist

Church, and was advised to 'ban the snake'.

This reaction had shades of Roman Catholicism. Our culture these days gives a physical interpretation to the myth that Saint Patrick banned snakes from Ireland, but in reality the story refers to the persecution and destruction of the beliefs of the Celtic shamans who flourished there before his arrival. The pattern repeats itself. However, with the hardest lessons comes the greatest learning, and in a strange way I knew that I had absorbed all that the Spiritualist movement could offer me.

I still occasionally attended a service and remained in touch with Lucy but I was still unaware that my greatest teachers were the unseen spirits that surrounded me, as once more I changed direction in my search. But I was finding an inner strength; I knew that my resolve would never waver and that, whatever befell me, I would continue my journey.

Chapter 7

THE MESSENGER BIRD

At this time I started to travel a great deal, seeking out ancient sites and 'power places'. Over the next three years I visited both Egypt and India several times. Always I was searching. Sometimes a series of almost unbelievable synchronicities would color my life, but I was looking for more: I wanted a repeat of the original six weeks and the mystical experiences that I had been dealt in the summer of 1990.

With one girl friend, who was an ardent Buddhist, I spent three weeks in Gangtok, Sikkim where the Dalai Lama was holding a Kalachakra Initiation. It was an arduous trip, but I really felt that here I might step once more into the mystical, paranormal realm that now seemed to be beyond my reach. It was a disappointing time, for of course this did not happen; I still had so much to learn about myself and there was a long way to go because at that time I was looking outside of myself for a connection to the mysteries.

In retrospect, however, I can see that this trip was an important part of my journey. There were in fact signposts everywhere, one of which made an impact on me, even though I failed to recognize it at the time. It was an introduction to the Maha Kala, a powerful Tibetan deity.

A picture hanging in the hallway of our hotel in Gangtok depicted the Buddhist representation of the Wheel of Life, but it was the fierce image at the top of the wheel that drew my attention. He was, I later learned, one of the so-called wrathful gods; he wore a headdress of skulls, and blood dripped from his fanged teeth and from the huge claws at the end of his four arms. His skin was jet black in color and he had three bulbous eyes, one

93

in the center of his forehead, but somehow I was drawn to him; I found it impossible to pass the image without stopping for several moments to gaze at it. Both the Hindu and Buddhist religions offer hundreds of gods to whom one can appeal and I could not understand my fascination for this one. He wasn't visually attractive like the popular goddess Tara – quite the opposite in fact.

There were many fierce and ancient pre-Buddhist gods of Tibet. The story is that the saint Padmasambhava subdued them by means of his magical powers and compelled them to watch over the Buddhist faith forever, as ferocious 'Protectors of the Dharma'. Maha Kala was one of these and was believed to embody time, especially time conceived as the inevitable destroyer of all things. Although his name means The Great Black One he is depicted in many forms with either six, four or two arms and can be white, black or red in colour, but always with the same three bulbous eyes. But for now I had no idea who was represented by the figure at the head of this picture. It would be another few years before I learned who this deity really was and came to know his true essence. As I proceeded to embrace the full power of this forceful entity, he would make a dramatic impact on my life.

The two weeks in Sikkim and the time spent in Delhi at the beginning and close of our trip were very interesting, but they were not providing the answers I was searching for and left me feeling somewhat deflated on my return to England. I knew Buddhism was not my path; it didn't pull at my heart strings and I had no desire to delve further into its doctrine. Indeed I felt certain I would not discover what I was looking for in India and vowed not to return to that country. However, I was not deterred in my quest and began to think about visiting the sacred sites in South America. I was going through a period when I thought I needed to detach myself from Western culture to discover some ancient and hidden knowledge. But before I could get there, I unexpectedly found myself returning to India.

An American woman named Janet, whom I had met in Egypt the year before, called to invite me to join a small group of people who were going to Ladakh. I fervently wished the trip had been heading in another direction, but in spite of misgivings I found myself immediately agreeing to go.

Janet's story was not uncommon. She had recently been divorced – behind her was a twenty-five-year marriage, but once the children were grown, her successful husband had gone through the 'midlife crisis' and turned his attention to a much younger woman. Janet was keeping herself occupied by going on every trip that presented itself and had swept me up to join her on this one.

The information about the trip was sketchy. An Indian woman living in Canada was organizing it and she had engaged an American man called John Perkins to travel with us and hold workshops as we moved through various places in India. Janet informed me that this man was a respected shaman and quite well known in her country. Although I didn't know what a 'shaman' was, it was the second time within days that this word had cropped up. I looked up the meaning in the dictionary and read, 'Priest of Shamanism, a religion of certain peoples of northern Asia based on belief in good and evil spirits who can be controlled only by shamans'. This vague information from the compiler really didn't help a lot. However, I felt drawn to the trip. The only prerequisite for it was to have read one of Mr Perkins books which, true to my upbringing, I purchased but placed unopened in my travel bag.

My husband and I had by now sold the big house in England and were living part of the time in Ireland. The week prior to my departure for this trip I was in that country, at our home out in the south west in a quiet and isolated corner of Kerry. After arranging to meet up with me in London on my return from India, my husband left on a business trip and I was at home alone.

This week would form a prelude to the mystical and magical events that would come to astound me on the forthcoming trip, for on each of the seven consecutive mornings prior to my departure I was given the most unusual and unsolicited alarm call. Every morning a continuous tapping on the bedroom window awakened me. The first two mornings, I got out of bed and drew back the curtains to see what the noise was, only to be confronted by a large black raven. He sat on the sill, quizzically tipping his head to one side, just looking at me, before flying off.

My explanation for this behavior was that the bird was probably confused by his reflection. But as he continued to reappear each morning, come rain or shine, I dismissed this idea. One morning I was already awake with the curtains open, and still he came and tapped away, peering in at me as I sat in bed drinking my morning cup of tea. He was not a bird common to the area, for the house is on the coast where the mountains seem to rise straight out of the sea, and the terrain is barren with very few trees.

Here I was in the wilds of Kerry, with my nearest neighbor living a quarter of a mile away. That week, our car had been parked outside his door while the entrance and driveway to our property were being resurfaced. The day came when I collected it to drive to the airport on the first stage of my journey to India; as I got into it, this neighbor, Mike, threw in a casual remark.

'Your car's been receiving a lot of attention this week. A large black-colored bird has insisted on sitting on it. He wasn't interested in either my car or my wife's – and they were parked alongside. And as fast as we shooed him off, he'd return. It was very strange.'

The comment registered because of the morning visits I had received from probably the same bird, but I gave it no further thought.

On the plane to Delhi I finally opened the John Perkins book.

It was titled *Shape Shifting* and I began by reading the few words offering a little of his biography. Thirty years before, as a member of the Peace Corps, John had been dispatched to the rainforests of Ecuador. Here he lived with the Shuar tribe and participated in their life, witnessing their earth-honoring ways and sustainable lifestyles. These fierce warriors, who own shrunken-head trophies but are also renowned as powerful healers, became his friends during the five years he spent with them. Returning from his tour of duty, he became immersed in a career as a consultant to the World Bank, but he always retained his contact with these people whom he had come to admire.

There came a point when John went through his own shape-shift. Inspired by the shamans of this tribe, he refocused the direction of his life. He founded an organization called Dream Change Coalition whose aim was to change corporate goals to make them more earth-honoring, to offer new sustainable ways of perceiving and working, and to encourage people to make their living through these means. This was his personal dream: a path he was energetically pursuing.

He had been trained by shamans both in the Andes and the Amazon and was now spending his life sharing the wisdom of these people with others. The word 'shaman' had only recently entered my vocabulary and at this point I knew nothing about Shamanism.

Once on the flight, I settled down to read the book, and one hour into the journey I knew that my patience over the past years was finally being rewarded, for the book tells of this man's personal experience of witnessing transformations. This was what I read:

... initiates into shape-shifting often begin by being the snake and shedding their old skins – this technique has been practiced for as long as human history has been recorded. It is a time for leaving behind fears, forgetting the hierarchal concepts schools have drummed into us.

The snake is a primal teacher so powerful that every major non-ecstatic religion has been threatened by it – the snake's power is recognized by nearly all shamanic cultures.

I couldn't believe what I was reading! This man was telling me that what I experienced during the energy shift into a snake in that suburban house nearly four years ago was understood and accepted by the Shuar. He wrote that their shamans can become, for a brief period, either a snake or a jaguar.

As well as describing cellular shape-shifts, this beautiful book also gave insight into the importance of transformation on a mental and emotional level. He described how, through ritual and ceremony, we can be guided into finding the ability to enhance our lives, to find our true purpose, and thereby enrich both our lives and the lives of those we touch. I was astounded at what I read, and as if to add to the authenticity of these words, they were found on page 108 of that edition. One hundred and eight happens to be the number of beads in the Tibetan prayer *mala* – a type of rosary – and is considered by Buddhists of that tradition to be a most powerful number.

At that moment my feelings were a combination of joy and relief. It was like a homecoming merged with the excitement of knowing I was at long last about to meet someone who understood what I had experienced. It was an 'end-of-term feeling', as if I had passed my first lot of exams and was now being given a glimpse of the future: ahead lay untold opportunities to learn and progress. A new adventure was awaiting me.

I found my way to the very large modern hotel in Delhi where the rest of the group, coming from the United States and Canada, would be gathering on this first leg of our trip. As I checked myself in, the clerk handed me a note which said we would all join for our first meeting at 10.00am the following morning and gave the room number where we would meet. Janet had not yet arrived and I had never met any of the other people who would be sharing this journey, so I simply took a walk around the hotel grounds, then had dinner by myself and went to bed early.

Sometime in the night I woke up, and as I did so, I heard the click of a door shutting. In that moment I knew without question that John Perkins, the first shaman I was ever to meet, had arrived. In this hotel with over two hundred rooms there was no doubt in my mind that he had just entered the room next door.

In the morning as I stepped out of the room to go down for breakfast, with beautiful precision the door to the adjacent room also opened and a figure emerged. It was that of a tall, lean man and I recognized the face from the flyleaf of the book I had been reading: it was John Perkins. This was the man whom the universe had arranged for me to meet, the man who would introduce me to Shamanism, and the man who would in the next few years assist and guide me through many initiations. I introduced myself and we walked down to breakfast together.

That morning I met for the first time the woman who had organized the trip; her name was Sheena Singh, an Indian artist now living in Canada. This trip was her inspiration; she had been at one of John's workshops in Florida the previous year and had said to him, 'Why don't you do a trip through India doing workshops at some of the most sacred places?'

His response had been, 'It's your dream. You organize it and I'll be there.'

This is exactly what she had done and now she was sharing her story of how it had all come together, a story that tells of multiple synchronicities.

Our group totaled twenty-nine people and was multicultural, composed of a mix of Indians, Americans and Canadians, with me as the lone European. For me it was a perfect introduction to Shamanism as these people came from backgrounds similar to mine; they held responsible jobs and were very grounded adults.

I was new to it all, but felt comfortable and safe as I was introduced over the next two weeks to the art of 'journeying' and to participation in rituals and ceremonies, most of which were performed to the accompaniment of drumming. John was the experienced leader, assisted by Sheena and an American woman named Eve Bruce. Their drums and sacred artifacts were the most precious part of their luggage.

There are a few people who pass through our lives who we recognize as truly remarkable; Eve Bruce is one I feel blessed to know. She is not only a qualified medical doctor but also a general and plastic reconstructive surgeon with a large practice in the Baltimore/Washington area. Her book *Shaman, M.D.* tells her story, but at this time when I first met her, it was yet to be written.

Andean shamans recognized her as someone special when she first visited them and they invited her to stay and study their healing techniques with them. She was the first non-Quechua woman to be inducted into the circle of Yatchaks, the name given to the 'Birdmen' of the Andes. This is an honor rarely extended by these powerful shamans. Her initiation into this elite group involved a ritual in a cave behind one of the sacred waterfalls, a spot where ten people had died in recent years whilst participating in ceremonies. Eve and I were the only grandmothers in the group, a fact that helped our bonding, for we were both unlikely candidates in this search for an unseen world.

We spent only one day in Delhi before returning to the airport and departing for Ladakh, where we arrived weary but excited at our hotel in Leh. The building was very attractive and of typical Ladakhi architecture: glistening white stone with red- and black-painted fretwork. It was surrounded by towering mountains, but there was a small shrub-filled garden with a stream, making a sheltered and peaceful oasis.

We picked up our keys. As this was my first of such trips, I had opted to room alone and was directed out of the main building to a long, low, single-story building of about nine rooms at the back, accessed by a small path; my room was number 1, right at the very end.

I have spent many nights alone in houses – it is not something that bothers me – but when I first entered my room here, I felt uneasy. It was nothing I could pinpoint, but anxiety struck me the moment I stepped through the door.

The room was very large, rectangular in shape, with the en-suite bathroom to the right as you entered; there was a small window on each of two sides and a pair of single beds at the far end. The only other furniture consisted of a small wardrobe and a chest of drawers, both of which looked a bit lost in this large room. The furnishings were a bit gloomy – dark wood and a dark-green carpet – but everything was spotlessly clean, so I pushed the uncomfortable feeling away, unpacked, and went out to find the others.

There were times during the first few days of this journey when I felt like an imposter. Everyone else seemed to understand what John was talking about as he spoke of spirits and 'soul loss' and spiritual 'tools'. As I listened I discovered that most of the group members seemed to have a career in one of the healing arts or had a lot of experience and knowledge of the other unseen worlds. I knew that the job I had done, namely raising a family while aiding and supporting my husband, was a worthy and valuable occupation. Yet when the others asked what I did, my response – 'I'm a housewife and mum' – seemed irrelevant.

However, as the first few days passed, I had a growing awareness that my place on this trip had been earned, that I was exactly where I should be. I was learning a great deal, but more than that, I felt I was rediscovering knowledge that had been buried somewhere deep within me.

We traveled around the area in a convoy of five large Land Rovers and one day took a trip out to the distant Hemis monastery. This was far up in the mountains along precarious single-file dirt tracks where the unguarded edge fell away into a sheer drop; after the first hour, there were only occasional passing places but fortunately we met no other traffic. The pass we were heading for is open for only a short time each year and the Hemis monastery is regularly cut off by the heavy snowfalls. The mountains here are totally barren but dramatic and beautiful, for the rocks seem to contain a variety of shades from soft pink to deep purple and black.

On reaching our destination, we made our way into the main courtyard where we were greeted by one of the resident lamas. He welcomed us and told us that most of the monks were absent – they had trekked higher into the mountains to perform the practice of *tumo*, which is the art of generating inner heat. The monks wrap their bare bodies in wet sheets and, using only their minds, are able to generate a body heat that not only stops them from freezing but dries the sheets. This practice has been witnessed and filmed, and it is awesome to see the steam begin to rise as these monks sit cross-legged in the snow, deep in meditation.

The monastery seemed to cling on to the side of the mountain and gave us the sense of being in an airplane, for the view from every part of it was closer to the clouds than to the valley floor thousands of feet below us. We all walked along the line of prayer wheels, holding our hands out to spin them as we passed, an action familiar to us now, after visiting several other temples in the Leh area since our arrival.

The lama then guided us to the main temple, which was dominated by a towering gilt-painted statue of the Buddha. It was a large rectangular room with a high ceiling and supporting pillars; the only natural light came from the huge double doors through which we had entered, but flickering around the deity's feet were the lights from many small butter lamps. The stone pillars that supported the roof held the remnants of red and blue paint, the last vestige of what were at one time highly colored decorative paintings, and there were ancient tankas hanging on the walls. On either side stood a double row of plain wooden benches; the surface of each had a glossy finish and the rounded edges that only come from much use.

There were several mats scattered on the uneven stone floor and a few very large cushions covered in a coarse and worn tapestry. The lama, who had graciously offered us the use of this special place to hold our ceremony, bowed deeply and departed.

John asked us to sit down, then explained what we would be doing. This exercise was called a 'retrieval', and our task would be to enter a meditative journey to find a 'power tool'. I listened carefully as he provided further information: the power tool we would find, he said, would not be for ourselves but for a partner. Once more I was entering a new experience and I felt thankful as several of the group expressed their ignorance of this exercise and raised their hands to ask questions, revealing that this was also the first time for them.

My partner was an Indian woman named Maya, one of Sheena's old school friends; she was most beautiful-looking and had a nature to match. Later, when we reached Dharamsala, strangers approached and spoke to her, and so we discovered that she was also a very well-known film actress.

John was clear in his instructions. After each of us had found a partner, we were to lie down side by side, making sure that the length of our bodies from shoulder to ankle was in close contact. We would do the retrieval one at a time whilst our partner remained unmoving and passive. The 'working' half of the duo would then mentally go on a journey, traveling in the imaginal world along whatever route appeared, on the search for a spiritual tool for the other person.

We were advised that this tool could be either animate or inanimate; it could be anything – absolutely anything. When we came upon this object we were to ask the question 'Are you the tool belonging to …?', mentally inserting the name of our partner We were told that most often the first answer is 'Yes' but if it came back as 'No' we were to continue the search until we received a positive 'Yes'.

John assured us that this tool was always there waiting to be claimed and it would be only a matter of minutes before it revealed itself to us. I felt a little worried and sensed a ripple of disbelief run through the group, but he ignored this and continued his instructions.

'When you have established that this tool is the one for your partner, I want you to reach up with both hands, take it, and pull it into your heart. Then sit up, and whilst your partner is still lying down, cup your hands and blow it into their heart.

'Next, I want you to gently help your partner up into a sitting position and again with cupped hands blow the object into the crown of their head. Sheena, Eve and I will be drumming all of the while this exercise is continuing.

'Please sit quietly and do not speak until everyone has performed this task. Then you can share the experience before we settle back and repeat it for the other half.'

It seemed a very responsible task so it was with some trepidation that I set off as the first to retrieve the power tool. It was an awesome setting, however, and this allowed me to forget that I was lying on a thin dusty mat on a stone-flagged floor. The gentle beat of three drums rapidly took my mind away from the physical; it truly 'journeyed' to a different place, and very quickly a picture formed. It was that of a young boy bearing a red velvet cushion, and lying on this cushion was an elephant tusk. He just appeared in front of me and, extending his arms, held out this gift. It was very clear and had happened extremely fast, but I remembered the instruction.

'Is this the tool for Maya?' I asked.

There was no doubt; a sense of the affirmative was immediate. I reached out, and was aware that I bowed before the cushion with the tusk reclining on it, before it was passed to me.

I completed the rest of the ritual and then sat there totally amazed and somewhat stunned, for what John had foretold had happened exactly. I was only vaguely aware of the others as slowly they completed the task: one half of each pair reached up and retrieved an unseen object, before ritually passing it on to the rightful owner.

In the brief time before the last person sat up I pondered on the fact that there had been only one tusk. I searched my recollection of the vision to make sure there had not been two, but there had not, and it was impossible to conjure up a second one. At this point the drumming came to a halt. Now we could share with our partners the result of our journey and reveal the image of the tool.

My partner sat there expectantly and it was with great relief that I was able to pass on the image of what I had collected. The sense of wonderment that encompassed me was doubly increased as she gasped on hearing what her spirit tool was.

'Oh! I can't believe that – it's Ganesh!' she exclaimed. 'He's such an important deity in my life.'

This elephant deity is one of the more popular gods in the Indian pantheon and although I was not aware of the mythology behind it and had never looked at it closely, I had been vaguely aware of the image on my previous trips to India.

'But there was only one tusk,' I apologized, feeling as if I had inadvertently mislaid one.

To my amusement and as confirmation that this was indeed a gift from the spirits, she said, 'But he only has one!'

It was wonderful. A short while later when our roles were reversed, she retrieved a first power tool for me. It was one that was to become a familiar object in my life; time and again over the years, this image would crop up when I most needed it. My tool was a full moon, but more than that, it was a full moon with its reflection shining on water – a beautiful image. However, it would be several years before I would learn the true significance of this gift when I finally discovered that this is the ancient symbol of the shaman.

Throughout the long journey back to Leh, I marveled at this

introduction to Shamanism and felt wave after wave of gratitude sweep through me.

There was no electric power during the nights in Leh; it was also sporadic during the day at the hotel and most evenings we had to rely on candles. It was on the third night of our stay here that I was exposed once more to the dark side of the other world.

There was a repetition of the terrorizing experience that had occurred at night several years before at my home in southern England. Again it was sometime in the middle of the night when I awoke, but this time the 'thing' was already present, not just in the process of arriving and slowly growing in a corner. It was there in the middle of the room, malevolent and terrifying. I lay there mentally demanding that it leave. This time there was no response. It remained in situ, huge and unmoving with an aura of evil.

It was as I became more alert that I realized I needed to use the bathroom, and I needed it badly. As the fear gripped me, so the pain in my bladder increased; there was no way I could wait much longer. Still the thing remained.

This was proving to be one the hardest tests I have ever had to face. I knew I had to get out of bed and walk towards this demon. There was no option; the only question was how long I could delay it. The choice was mine, for there was an innate knowing that my task was to find the courage, but this time the battle was more than a mental one. This time I was physically alone and it was a *huge* challenge. From somewhere deep inside me I understood that I had to step into this fear; I had to overcome it.

Finally I threw the covers back and ran towards the bathroom, fully expecting this area of pure evil to engulf me. I made it to the bathroom with great relief. Taking some huge deep breaths, I seriously debated whether to remain there for the night, for here I felt comparatively safe. I knew the evil energy remained in the center of the bedroom; although it had not grown larger or moved its position, it was without doubt still in the room.

Facing up to it had given me strength and taught me that if I could do it once then I could do it again. My sleep attire is of preference a white cotton nightdress so I groped in the darkness of the bathroom to find the single small towel to wrap around myself. The low temperature at night in Ladakh, spreading coldness through my body, gave me the added incentive. Fighting back the fear and the tears, I took a deep breath, moved out of the bathroom entrance and, almost flying across the room, threw myself into the bed. I was back! I felt safe. The evil entity was still there, but I knew in that instant that I was now the stronger one. It could no longer threaten me. It remained for several more minutes, then I sensed it dissipating, and finally it vanished.

The events of this night I kept to myself. I shared them with no one.

Later, on the following day, we went to visit a monastery. I was sitting in the jeep waiting for the rest of the group to return when I noticed from the window an area that the locals had used for burning rubbish. Spread out on the blackened and charred earth were some animal bones, but what I had particularly spotted was a sheep's skull with a pair of curly horns. Jumping from my seat, I hurriedly got out of the vehicle and walked towards it.

The flesh had been picked clean by the local vagrant dogs and the vultures, before the fire had cleansed the rest. As I stood looking down at the skull, I knew I needed it. Where do such thoughts come from? I gave no regard to what anyone else would think or say; some deep need overruled every rational thought. I bent down and carefully picked it up, then, removing a silk scarf from around my neck, I gently wrapped it around this precious object. I was so happy. I knew this was what was needed in my bedroom. With this in place, there would be no further intrusions.

Once the horns were installed on the window sill above my

bed, the hotel room immediately felt different. The sun was shining but it was more than that – the energy of the room had changed. I questioned my actions. How could I, a woman from such a grounded and materialistic background, be doing such things? But I was calmed by a deep-rooted acceptance that knowledge was bubbling up, coming from the experience of my incarnations many years ago. I felt serene.

As the journey progressed through Ladakh and back into India, it unfolded in many magical ways. We visited many temples and monasteries, some of which were far up in the mountains in very isolated locations, and as the days progressed I felt more and more fascinated by what we were doing. The internal search for spirit guides and power tools resonated and seemed to awaken some deep and long-hidden memories within me. Synchronicities abounded.

Then, about one week into our journey, came the day that would seal my belief in Shamanism and set the path for the rest of my life.

Without any planning on our part, we just happened to be in Leh on the same day that the Dalai Lama was holding an open-air meeting on the local playing field to celebrate the festival of Wesak. There were vast crowds of Indians and a great many Tibetans who had trekked for days just to spend a few hours listening to their much-loved and respected spiritual leader.

We had collected another member of our group on our arrival in Ladakh: a monk whose name was Lama Ji. He was a well-educated gentleman who originated from Ladakh and had spent a lot of time traveling between Buddhist monasteries in many countries. He spoke very good English and was accompanying us as our guide and source of knowledge.

Lama Ji had led us along to this meeting site. We had turned up on the off chance that we might see or hear something inter-esting, but after he spoke to the Tibetan organizers they graciously found our small band of Westerners a place very close to the podium and also generously shared *tsampa* (the traditional Tibetan drink) and sweetmeats with us. It was an extraordinary occasion and we appreciated how lucky we were to be present at such an auspicious time.

Wesak is the day when the birth, enlightenment and death of Buddha are celebrated as one event. This is the most important festival in the Buddhist calendar and is held at the time of the May full moon. In view of my dismissal of Buddhist beliefs and my reluctance to return to this part of the world where it is so entrenched, it is interesting to note that what turned out to be a momentous event in my life happened on this auspicious day.

This large open-air meeting was held in a convenient level space on the outskirts of the town; it was ringed by foothills, and beyond these towered the snow-covered Himalayan mountains. A small platform had been erected at one end of this area and here, on a simple stage of wooden planks with just a small canvas awning to protect him from the sun, sat the Dalai Lama.

This revered man, who talks continually with kings and presidents, also maintains a close connection with the common people and graciously accepts the unsought worship of the Tibetans. He is held in awe and high respect by the rest of the world and we, like everyone else, were content to sit in the dust at his feet. He is indeed a shaman of the highest order.

Here, on this makeshift stage, he spoke for about an hour in a language our small group could not comprehend, but it scarcely mattered. We had read his books and seen him on television, and his words of wisdom had touched us many times. The story of his exile from his homeland and the atrocities being perpetrated in Tibet were common knowledge. To sit in the vicinity of this man was a blessing. Such is his presence and charisma that we were oblivious to the heat and the dirt; there was an energy – a connection – that encompassed us all. The unspoken message was clear: our cultures may distinguish and divide us, but our souls bond and unite us as we seek the answers to the same questions.

Once His Holiness had finished speaking, the ceremony continued with music on both sitars and drums, as dancing girls garbed in traditional costume sprang from all corners. There were also Tibetan shamans adorned in multicolored ornate robes with scrying mirrors hanging from their belts, both men and women bearing the weight of heavy headdresses studded with turquoise beads. Swathes of saffron and gold color threaded through this multitude as many monks weaved their way through the crowds, trying to get closer to the Dalai Lama. The whole event saturated my senses as the sun beat down. My nostrils were filled with the smells of it all: a pot-pourri of myth and magic.

The hospitality of these people then reached its height. I have witnessed many times on my travels that the fewer material possessions people own, the more giving and generous is their nature, and so it was here: to our amazement, through the vast crowd came a group of monks, offering a sweet biscuit and a drink of tsampa to every single person gathered there.

After this memorable morning we were scheduled to continue our journey. As the celebration came to a close, we departed from the site and, with Lama Ji leading the way, slowly walked a mile or so to the home of a local shaman who had agreed to meet with us. We arrived at the shaman's house ahead of her but were informed she was on her way, so we stood around waiting and talking about the event we had been fortunate enough to attend.

It was not long before she arrived: an attractive Tibetan woman, probably in her late thirties, accompanied by her husband, her mother and two small children. She was dressed in her very best garments: the beautiful embroidered traditional Tibetan robes. On her head she wore the prized *peyrak*, a cobra-shaped headdress studded with turquoise stone and red coral; she had of course been participating in the Wesak celebration and honoring the Dalai Lama.

She was profuse in her apologies for keeping us waiting, placing her hands together and making innumerable deep low bows. She ushered us all into her small sitting room; there were so many of us that we were happy to sit on the floor, but she bustled about finding us cushions and making sure we were comfortable, then excused herself to prepare tea for everyone.

Lama Ji said, 'Her name is Tsering Dolma. She is the Ladakhi oracle and is recognized as a very powerful shaman.' He was able to translate from Tibetan into Hindi; Sheena would then assist in converting the language to English, a system that had so far worked well. This gracious hostess was visually the most unlikely image of the archetypal shaman, but Lama Ji was a quiet and wise man and not given to overstatement.

Within a short time, tea had been served and our hostess had changed out of her ornate gown into something less precious. With her mother she joined us and we watched closely as she made preparations. In a small area at one side of the room was a low table with some bowls and bells on it; she sat down behind this, and her mother, who was carrying a small bag, seated herself alongside. Methodically this table was transformed into an altar as the shaman requested items, one by one, which her mother produced out of the bag. Occasionally she would look at the item and return it to her mother, requesting something else.

Our lama informed us that this setting-up was part of the ritual and preparation, but all the while the shaman was communicating with her spirit guides and when everything was ready she would complete her ceremonial dressing and go into trance.

This trance state was something I had read about but never witnessed and there was an air of expectancy as we sat quietly watching. The shaman donned a small crown-shaped hat; she poured what looked like brown sugar into one of the bowls, rice into another container and what looked like water into a third. Every so often she would pick up one of the small brass bells and ring it loudly, calling out something as she did. There was also another instrument she would pick up and use briefly before replacing it on the table. This was a *damaru*: a small double-sided drum on a stick, about four inches in diameter with a bead attached to a cord hanging on either side. The shaman used a wrist action to rotate and reverse it; as she did so, the beads hit the drum with a rapid but distinctive sound. All of her actions were performed with reverent attention and in a very ritualistic manner.

Her mother was vigilant, watching closely. She reminded me of an altar server playing his part in relation to the priest in a Catholic mass.

Then the shaman began to yawn. She made several huge deep-breath yawns with her mouth stretching widely; as the yawning increased, her chest expanded and before our eyes she seemed to grow in stature. After a few moments her mother spoke a few words and our lama said quietly, 'The deity has arrived.'

We were then each invited, one at a time, to present ourselves to the shaman, to ask a question requesting help with any problem, either physical or emotional, or to ask for a direct healing. I was fascinated by it all and could not move my eyes from an engrossed observation of everything taking place. In turn my companions shuffled across the room and one at a time moved themselves in front of her. It was a laborious process because of the language difficulties; occasionally Lama Ji, Sheena and the attendant mother were all involved in the interpretation.

There were different spirits moving through the physical body of the shaman. As they changed, renewed drumming and a different chant welcomed the new entity. Through our mediators a variety of questions were asked. Most people asked for help with medical problems, all of which were dealt with in a similar manner: the shaman took a small metal pipette and placed it directly onto the patient's skin – sometimes on the chest or stomach, sometimes on the back – and then she sucked. At no time was the skin broken, but as she removed the pipette from her mouth, she placed her finger over the top, momentarily holding the contents inside the 'straw', in the same way that a child plays with a lemonade straw. Then, reaching for a bowl, she released the fluid into it.

I was in pole position, sitting right next to her, and I nearly gagged as I saw the bowl start to fill: from most of the members of our group she extracted a dark-brown slime. From some it appeared to be congealed blood; from yet another individual she produced a stone that 'pinged' as it hit the side of the bowl. At no time did she drink anything and there was no sign of her regurgitating.

It was mind boggling. This person who an hour ago had arrived as an attractive, laughing woman had transformed into something else. The woman had disappeared and in her place was a powerful deity performing extractions.

There was one healing that removed all skeptical doubt from me. One member of our flock was a very heavy smoker who 'lit up' at every opportunity. For the past couple of hours she had had no opportunity to indulge this habit and her request to the shaman for healing was unrelated, for she was seeking help by asking for guidance in a difficult relationship. The shaman requested that she turn around and, placing the pipette on the skin of her back directly in line with her lungs, drew off a substance that looked exactly like tar. Again and again she repeated this action. The substance stuck both to the bowl and the metal straw, so much so that she dispensed with that implement and used a fresh one on the next client.

Then it was my turn. I had no immediate problems of either a physical or an emotional nature. My request was that the deity would give me guidance on my spiritual path.

This request was relayed to the shaman. As I bowed in front of her and got to my knees, I immediately felt myself begin to shake. I tried to straighten up but uncontrollable tremors rippled through me; I was aware of where I was but my physical body seemed to belong to someone else. The shaking became quite violent, then suddenly the visual image of a Tibetan deity filled my head. I threw back my head, and strange sounds came out of my mouth, like a war cry. It was not a shout, but rather a burst of strange words in a language unfamiliar to me.

My hands started to make gestures with strong, positive actions, somewhat like a semaphore message. I could feel and see my body performing, but there was an overwhelming sensation of being detached from the physical part of myself, a feeling as if I was merely an observer.

I suppose this lasted a few minutes; it's hard to say. Then I felt something raining down on me; as my consciousness reunited with my physical body, I became aware that the 'rain' was rice. It was hitting me and scattering around. The shaman was throwing the rice and I felt this was being done as a blessing; she was taking handfuls of it from a bowl and tossing it into the air above my head. As it peppered me, I felt a movement of the powerful and unexpected energy that had filled me; it shifted and flowed out of me. The feeling as it left was very physical; there was the sensation of a fluid-like motion leaving my body.

Silently I knelt there, feeling very tired. Then the mother spoke and our interpreter passed the message to me, quietly saying, 'Go carefully to your seat.'

Moving away, I carefully sat down to one side with my back against the wall. One of the shaman's small daughters immediately came across and sat on my lap, and the proceedings continued as before.

I sat there in that room trying hard to rationalize what had occurred. This had been utterly unexpected and unreal, and was far removed from my life in England. My family thought I had come to India as a tourist, which indeed was my original intent, but so many unusual things had occurred leading up to this trip that I had already sensed it would be much more than that. There was a deep innate knowing within me, and although these events were very bewildering, I had a feeling that a veil was being lifted.

As I sat quietly with the small child on my lap, the healings continued with the rest of the group; no one else exhibited a reaction such as mine. Then, without warning and for no obvious reason, an image suddenly came into my mind: I was transported back to Sikkim, to the hotel in Gangtok and the picture of the Maha Kala. The image of this fearsome deity came in out of nowhere and filled my head.

Upon the completion of the healings, the deities departed from the physical body of the shaman and there was a tangible shift of the atmosphere in the room. It was like watching a layer of this woman being removed – a distinct peeling away – and then the jovial housewife re-emerged. She got to her feet, smiling at us, and left the room.

We each discreetly placed a few dollars on the side of the altar, posed outside for a group photo with the shaman in the center, then, giving our thanks both to her and her family, we left.

It was my first experience of such a powerful force and I had no comprehension of what had happened. The shaman made no comments to me personally about what had occurred, and as we emerged from her house no one remarked on my behavior. The only mention of the incident came later from Janet, who told me there had been several villagers squeezed into the back of the room where she was sitting by the door, and when I first let out the cries they had leapt backwards. However, they relaxed as they witnessed the mother of the shaman break into a smile; this protective assistant started to rock herself backwards and forwards with immense pleasure, and this action seemed to reassure the onlookers; from then on, an atmosphere prevailed where all present felt they were privileged witnesses.

I was so new to Shamanism that in my innocence I assumed the behavior I had shown was probably a regular occurrence. My companions, I would later understand, were as bewildered as I and thought I had the answers! Now I understand that when occurrences such as these happen there is no rational answer and that to seek one is irrelevant. The answer, if there is one, has to come from inside the individual.

For me it was an experience that was both frightening and bewildering. But always I maintained a deep-rooted belief that it was an event I needed to accept and honor, an event that I must not dissect with logical reasoning.

Chapter 8

MEETING THE DALAI LAMA

Back at the hotel I showered and then as looked at myself in the small mirror I became aware that something was odd, the reflection looking back at me was somehow different.

It was certainly me, but there was an element in what I was seeing that was not the same.

At first I wasn't sure what it was, but after many years of daily viewing I knew there was something, as I took a closer look, I did a 'double take'. It must be the light I thought as I tilted my head at all angles. Then I went over and picked up the magnifying make-up mirror from where it was laid on the bed and walked across to the window.

It was hard to believe, but there was no mistake and it was no trick of the light.

My eyes had changed color!

All of my life they had been brown with flecks of green. Now as I fixated my focus on this reflection I saw they were predominantly green with flecks of brown.

I was stunned.

As I dressed I repeatedly picked up the small mirror and re-checked, there was no mistake. It was impossible to concentrate on anything else and I anxiously waited our pre-dinner meeting in order to share this bizarre occurrence with my fellow travelers.

Most of the group were already there and sat quietly when I arrived and the moment I sat down I blurted out, "My eyes have changed color".

John looked up at me and then posed the question, "What color have they changed to?"

Having received the answer he turned to Lama Ji who although not partaking in any of our workshop activities would always be around and sit discreetly to one side where he would silently observe everything.

He had also been with us all day and witnessed the trance state I had fallen into that afternoon.

'Lama Ji, is this possible?" John asked.

The Lama peered at me and said, "Ah, Yes. This is possible."

That was it. The subject was then closed.

Shamans, Lamas and Holy Men accept without question many of the world's mysteries.

This was a cellular shape shift, a visual proof that we are, as the scientists claim composed of millions of molecules and atoms; we are an energy that is constantly flowing and changing.

There was to be a second visit to a different Tibetan shaman a couple of days later and this time I was determined to remain in the background and merely observe, it was all getting too much and the rational part of my brain that had dominated my life until this point was getting hammered.

Once again it was a female shaman and her name was Abbi Llamo, this lady was much older than the first shaman we had visited and this time she had gone through the ritualistic procedure of entering the trance in private. We had waited out of sight in an adjoining room from where we could clearly hear the sound of her drums, bells and chanting.

When she was ready to receive us her husband gave the signal and silently beckoned to us with his finger and we slowly filed past him into the small back room where we got our first glimpse of her. This lady shaman was dressed in ornate and ancient colorful robes and also was wearing a small red and blue bead embroidered crown type head dress that had long ribbons hanging from it.

Her nose and mouth were covered with a cotton scarf that tied at the back. This regalia was undoubtedly important and beautiful but it was her eyes that I was immediately drawn, they were dark and bird like and intensely penetrating, she covered the room glancing at each one of us and as her eyes met mine it felt as if she was looking directly into my soul.

We all seated ourselves on the floor and once we had settled quietly the healings commenced. Again, as with our visit to the previous shaman this was not done in any set order but one by one as they felt drawn my companions in turn moved to a position in front of her to receive a healing.

This shaman used no pipette and there were no visible extractions, instead she muttered incantations and moved her hands around close to their body and would occasionally appear to pluck something invisible from the person knelt before her. Each healing was concluding by her tying a piece of string either around their waist or finger and giving them instruction to wear it continually for a certain length of time and this varied between anything from a day to a week.

Through our two translators we learned that she was telling one man in our group that he had a problem in his home in the USA and she lifted a cloth bag from her side and removed a small item that I was unable to see which she then wrapped and then tied into a small parcel advising him to place it in a cavity in the wall of his home when he returned.

There were twenty seven of, sat of us in any space we could find on the floor of this small room, there had been no lineal order to the healings and today I was only watching, fascinated by it all but resolved to only be an observer with no plan to receive a healing.

It was then time to leave and Sheena asked "Anyone else?"

I sat quietly.

The shaman turned and said something to Lama Ji who then spoke to Sheena.

Glancing around the room Sheena looked directly at me.

"She wants to see you Wendy", she said.

Shaking my head I declined but the shaman spoke again and Lama Ji said,

"Please come forward".

Reluctantly I got up to my feet and stepped through my companions as I go in front of her I took a deep breath and bowed then kneeled down in front of her.

The shaman half turned and reaching behind produced a large silver sword which she then draped a colored silk scarf over the hilt before indicating to me to lower my head as I followed her instruction she began to chant and wave the sword in a series of distinct and symbolic gestures.

This second time for me with a shaman was very different, in spite of this fearsome weapon being waved in close proximity to my head it all felt very peaceful and relaxing, she then gently replaced the sword behind her and as I looked up I saw she had taken a length of rag into which she was twisting several grains of rice. This rag she tied around my neck and through our interpreter I was ordered to not remove it for three days and as an added protection she tied a piece of red string around one of my fingers again with instructions to not remove it, it was to remain until it fell off. This piece of string stayed on my finger for over three months and eventually felt off in a sacred site at an auspicious time.

There was no fixed schedule to our travels journey through India and Ladakh and they took on a momentum of its own.

Sheena as the facilitator of the trip failed to provide any structure and every day the plans changed, but the whole trip had a feeling of orchestration that was beyond any human input. Everything seemed to be happening exactly as it should and in exactly the right moment, there was a oneness with the Universe and I flowed with it

A few days later we left Leh en route for Dharamsala by 'coincidence' we found ourselves on the same small plane as His Holiness the Dalai Lama.

The flight would be short and we persuaded John to approach the Dalai Lama's secretary and ask if it was possible for him to speak to his Holiness, this was such an opportunity to convey our thanks for the hospitality of the Tibetan people, at our good fortune to be able to listen to him talking and for the blessings bestowed on us all at the Wesak ceremony. Such a moment could not be missed and we knew it would be regretted if he arrived back in America having let it pass.

John sat back in his seat; the secretary had said he would come back and take John forward to His Holiness if he so agreed, we were not very hopeful but at least we had tried

Half way through this short flight the message arrived and we saw John get up and walk forward. We strained our necks but the curtain swished back protecting this private area and John vanished behind it. Some fifteen minutes later he re-emerged and looking somewhat stunned and bemused made his way back to his seat.

Like Chinese whispers, "What did he say? What did he say?" ran from seat to seat.

Then back came the answer, the Dalai Lama has offered to give our group a private audience on probably the day after tomorrow.

It was unbelievable! This man's diary is filled months in advance, but he was making room for us!

But there was yet more to come.

At the airport we got on to a coach to complete the journey to our Hotel in Dharamsala. John waited until we had left the city behind and were driving through the beautiful countryside beginning our climb into the foothills of the Himalayas and he then reached over and took the microphone.

'Well", he began "This journey gets more incredible by the day. Is is impossible to quantify the odds of us being the same place as the Dalai Lama without having made an effort of any description to tie in with his schedule. All we had ever done was to hope that he would be in residence at his

Monastery in Dharamsala at the same time as we were in the town.

To find ourselves in Leh when he was giving unpublicized teachings which we managed to attend was a special gift.

To share the same small airplane makes it Synchronistic.

To have the opportunity to speak to him on behalf of us all and now to be granted an audience with him puts it almost beyond belief"

Our heads were reeling as the magnitude of these odds revealed themselves, but John's next sentence knocked our socks off.

He continued "When I got level with him he put aside a book he was reading"

As he spoke I was aware the enormity of what he was about to divulge had left him stunned.

"I know it sounds unbelievable" he paused "but he was reading one of my books. He was reading Shape Shifting"

This drew gasps from everyone on the coach, but from none more than those emitted by me for he was referring to a copy of the self same book that I was carrying in my luggage, the very same book whose words had shone a light in my darkness.

The Universe works in mysterious ways, it's magic to perform. Never had these words been more apt.

After the many years of serving a lonely apprenticeship, of continually seeking and longing to learn it felt as if I had finally reached a platform and during the time we traveled through Ladakh I embraced this new exposure to shamanism.

The shamanic area was all untested ground for me and although for several years I had been experiencing many things that were paranormal, my learning had all mostly been done in isolation for no guru or teacher had appeared to guide or assist me. Every step of the way I had had to rely on my own innate wisdom, in truth as I had now discovered by listening to John I had without being aware of their presence or giving them credit actually been listening all the time to my spirit guides and in particular to my maternal grandmother, a lady who had died when I was seventeen but I often thought about.

Everything John said felt so comfortable and with hind sight it is easy for there had been a sign almost from the beginning of the role ancestors play in our lives.

But there was still more to come and the gift of another big shift in the right direction would come after we arrived in Dhahamsala for it was there that I took my first shamanic journey and what started out as a guided meditation turned into so much more.

We were staying at a small comfortable Hotel where we were continuing with the workshop and our first morning session was held in a large room on the ground floor; here John introduced us to the practice of 'journeying' which for me was a first time and proved to be a very enjoyable experience.

This trip had now provided me with an entry into the shamanic route to find a connection to our individual spirit guides, to our power animals and to the tools that offer us help in connecting to other realities. I was finding it fascinating and it all felt very comfortable and reassuring.

There was a sense that this was all so right, a feeling that at last I was on the right track and there was a purpose in all the metaphysical events that had spun me around over the past few years.

I was looking forward to the afternoon session and this time we gathered outside on a large terrace which ran the width of the building.

The Hotel was set on the side of a mountain and at one end of this terrace was a small gate which led on to a small rough grassed level area whilst a three foot wall contained the terrace and protected the unwary for the other end of the terrace dropped down two stories.

We arranged ourselves in a large circle, the sun was shinning and the day was warm and still and I hung my cotton shawl over the wall behind me and leaned back against it.

There were many huge black birds circling overhead and there was a discussion going on about the association of ravens and crows who in many cultures are deemed to be magical.

I recall asking Lama Ji, "Why are they doing this? Does it have any meaning or significance?"

He had looked at me deeply and affirmed the comments of my companions.

"Ah yes. The raven has long been known as the sacred messenger"

At that moment although at present unknown to me, this would be proven within hours of my return to the West and in the heart of London I would be shown how this mysterious bird continues to perform its role.

These birds were directly overhead and they continually turned and floated lifted on the air thermals generated by the terrain, they remained in this same spot and appeared to be watching us.

John began the afternoon workshop by reminding us to draw on the images we had visualized during the morning's work. These, and he emphasized his words, were our guides and guardians, they had drawn close and made us aware of their presence in order to help us. He urged us to grow familiar with them, to build a partnership with them, to learn to trust and listen to the advice they gave us. He added that in the many years he had been working with his guides, they had never let him down and on the rare occasions when he had failed to heed them he had always come to regret it this afternoon we would continue on a similar theme with our learning and practice.

Drums hold an important place in shamanic work and whilst the other participants and I had been journeying John, Eve and Sheena had provided the drumming. This beat that resonates with the heart and echoes the beat of our planet Earth aids the shift of our consciousness into other realities; it moves us from the focus of our immediate surroundings and helps the transition through the thin veil that divides the realms.

Our group quieted down and we made ourselves comfortable, our facilitators began a gentle drumming and this time John had directed us to look to the future to see where our journey through life was taking us.

As I closed my eyes I began the search for one of my guides or a power animal to accompany me. There was no immediate sense that they were close and instead of the usual anticipatory feeling of something good on its way I felt somewhat uncomfortable, not in a physical sense but more on an emotional level.

"Just close your eyes and go with the rhythm", were Johns instructions," See where it takes you"

I had been meditating on and off for a few years now and had no reason to expect that today the experience would be any different.

But immediately I closed my eyes I seemed to leave the terrace and my surroundings and I began to feel anxious as if I was moving into something I wished to avoid. I pulled myself back and opened my eyes and looked around. Everything was the same as it had been a few minutes earlier, my companions were sat peacefully, relaxed and eyes closed, the sun was shinning and all was normal and exactly the same as it had been moments ago. I leaned back with my eyes open and John spotted me and as he walked over still rhythmically beating his drum, he raised his eyebrows questioningly as he bent towards me.

"I think I'll sit this one out" I whispered.

"Try again" he responded and reluctantly but obediently I closed my eyes.

Instantly there was a darkness that I had not experienced before and it felt as it something was closing in on me. My legs went out in front of me as I felt myself sliding forward and moving from a sitting position into a half lying one. This did not feel good and I tried to shift the level of consciousness and open my eyes, but there was a force pressing down on me, a huge weight.

I was vaguely aware of the sound of the drums but it was impossible to open my eyes I was totally unable to lift my eyelids. I made a supreme effort to sit back up and as I did so I felt something being thrown over my head and a cloth was now covering me.

At this moment I felt myself falling rapidly into a black abyss. Nothing could stop me.

I was falling, falling, falling.

As I did so these brilliant flashes of scenes appeared before me, but more than that an enormous sense of loss swept over me. I experienced pain and anguish like I had never felt before.

With the first flash I saw a very large book; it was similar to a medieval Bible with gold trimmed pages and appeared to be made of leather with metal edges to the cover. There was something written on the outside, like a title but in a strange language that I failed to recognize.

However I knew without doubt this was an important and treasured book that contained secret and Sacred writings. The importance of this book was paramount, this sense of this struck me with an almost physical force

Next I saw myself entering a cave, but knowing at the same time that this was not the first time I had been there I was actually returning to it. Inside to the left was a stone table and I knew this was where the book should lay but the book was missing........the stone lay bare.

This was when I fell into panic; I knew this book was full of powerful knowledge that was of immense importance to the community. I knew I was the guardian of this Sacred book, a book that contained ancient wisdom and now it was missing, lost, gone forever.

The sense of loss, pain, guilt and anguish that rushed into me and filled me was intense.

It consumed me in the most indescribable way. It was a grief that was both emotional and physical, unbearable and I cried out with the pain of this loss. I screamed at the pain this loss was causing me.

Then as if through a mist I became vaguely aware of my immediate surrounding back on this terrace in Dharamsala.

I could hear distant voices.

One was saying, "What's happening to her?"

Then another female voice of authority demanded "Don't touch her!" Then someone was half holding me, picking me up and as if through a mist came John's question "Wendy, can you walk?"

My body felt like a rag doll and I was unable to answer.

I was aware of being half dragged half carried and then I was laid down. I felt the ground beneath me and the warmth of the sun baked earth on my back.

I heard Johns voice saying "Let it out. Let it all go".

Then from somewhere deep inside me came this scream.

A heart-rending scream came forth and reverberated off the surrounding mountains.

Three times came a scream that echoed the pain that emitted from me, the sound bounced off the mountains and reverberated around the valley.

I had no idea why it was doing this, the body was like an automaton, and the part of this body that was 'me' was stood to one side.

Slowly I opened my eyes. The tall figure of John Perkins was standing looking down at me, he was smiling "Take your time", he said. "Rejoin us when you are ready". Then turning he returned to the terrace.

I lay there feeling exhausted, aware that I was now outside of the area where my companions were gathered and I was laying down on the ground on a small level area of the mountain outside of the terrace.

The heat from the sun felt good as it warmed my body, but I felt exhausted and I made no attempt to move. There was a strange sense of all of the parts of me moving back together, reassembling themselves and once more becoming one cohesive unit.

It was impossible to make any sense of what had happened. There was nothing untoward when we had commenced this afternoon's workshop, nothing like this had ever happened to me before.

There was no denying that my beliefs over the past few years had changed dramatically from those that I had held for the many years preceding them. But I was still the archetypal grandmother when not traveling in my search for an understanding of the mysterious side of our lives and the majority of my days were conducted in a pattern similar to millions everywhere.

Now as I lay there on the dirt on this mountain in Northern India I tried to find some rational explanation for what had just occurred.

There was none.

It was all beyond me.

Slowly I sat up and looked around, and then cautiously I got to my feet. There was a dreamlike quality to all I was seeing, everywhere was quiet and peaceful, the drumming had ceased and there was no sound coming from the terrace. I glanced in that direction but from the angle where I was stood there was no sign of anyone.

Then as I stood there a most incredible thing happened, first one of the large black birds that had been flying high over our heads as we commenced our workshop alighted on the ground in front of me. It landed very close, at a distance of only ten feet or so away. He folded his wings and just stood there looking at me with bright beady eyes as I stood motionless and returned his gaze. To my amazement, there was a whoosh of wings and a second bird joined him, then another, and another,

within seconds there were eight or nine of these creatures gathered in front of me. None of them were pecking at the ground; all were quite still and facing me. It was bizarre. I stood there gazing back at them; they were large versions of the English raven, black and sleek. There was an instant connection through my eyes and theirs and into my head came this sense that they were communicating with me. We were on the same wavelength there was a form of telepathy running between these beautiful black birds and myself. There was nothing specific just an unquestioning knowing that we were indisputably linked.

I stood there mesmerized; it felt like I was half out of my body, stranding two worlds and standing with one foot each in a separate and very different world.

Then the spell was broken as a voice called out.

"Wendy, we are about to start again".

I looked across to where the shouting was coming from and one of my fellow participants, a man full of self-assurance, who was prone to organize us all, was stood up on the terrace waving to me to return.

The interruption was like a knife cutting through the rapport that I was sensing with these birds and at once with a great flapping of wings they all lifted off. I watched as they headed skywards seeking new thermals to take them back to their chosen view of the surroundings.

Obediently I turned towards the entrance to the terrace, I was experiencing a strange feeling of detachment and it still felt as if I was moving through a non-normal reality. As I walked the few steps back to join the group another scene flashed before me, so vivid and real. Clearly I saw in front of me the area where we were working only now it was a totally different scene from the one I had left only a short time ago

The scene that I had been carried from was full of color.

The floor of the terrace had rugs and cushions set out on top of the tiles. In the center we had defined a scared space where we had placed candles and flowers and added to this were items that we had individually laid there. There were a variety of things that had special significance for each of us, there were some stones and feathers, pieces of jewelry and small ornaments. Twenty-nine of us including the co ordinators were participating in this workshop and we had all been sat there with bags or bundles of some description, the area had been filled.

Now what I was suddenly visualizing was so very different.

I shivered for even the weather had dramatically and instantly changed. The sun had suddenly disappeared, there was a chill in the air and I saw the terrace was deserted, there was no sign of anyone and no trace that there had ever been any activity. The floor was dusty and unswept and in the center was a small collection of dried leaves that a cold wind was swirling in circles.

Into my head came the thought 'where has everyone gone?' all of this happened in seconds as I walked the few paces towards the surrounding wall. Then as I reached the small gate at the entrance I saw, everything was as it had been. Everyone was still sat down and listening as John sat to one side addressed them all, the workshop was still in progress. The vision of the empty terrace with the dusty swirling leaves had been vivid, as real as any experience.

I was stunned and speechless.

The events of the past fifteen minutes now left me feeling shocked and bewildered and totally confused.

I stood there waiting until John had finished talking, then walked into the circle and resumed the place I had recently vacated.

If I had been expecting an explanation for my behavior I would have been disappointed for none was forthcoming and for the time being I told no one of my visions or even mentioned how the birds that had been the objects of our earlier discussion had descended to my feet and communicated with me.

It would be a long time before I finally accepted that every life experience is our own personal learning and we must use our own innate wisdom to find an interpretation.

John did later ask what I had visualized during the trance and his only comment was "I was drumming so hard I broke the drumstick!" It substantiated my feeling that I had journeyed a long distance for I was unaware of any sound and had heard no drums.

It was a few days later that we congregated outside the gates of the Dalai Lamas base in Dharamsala and we were all buzzing with excitement.

Once through these gates and seated in a comfortable sitting room of his residence we were granted the privilege of a private audience.

This amazing man who in constantly in touch with state leaders and concerned with world affair spent forty minutes with our group, he retains a humility that has not removed him from the day to day basic needs and problems of the rest of us. The abiding memory of all that meet him is his sense of fun and his joy in life.

We had all purchased a Khata scarf in preparation for our visit and as our audience with his Holiness came to an end we each in turn filed up to him. Holding our forearms stretched out in front of us with the scarf draped across them he lightly placed his hand on our head as he blessed each of us individually, then lifting the scarf from our arms he gently placed it around our necks.

Outside he stood and posed for a group photo of us all wearing our identi- kit new scarves.

What an incredible memento to take back to our homes.

This was our last day in Dharamsala and after our meeting we walked a short distance to the abode of another respected Tibetan Lama this was a man who had if fact been a tutor to his

Holiness many years ago. Here in his home we participated in and were blessed with yet another memorable ceremony, where the Lama called on healing energies of Green Tara to be bestowed on us.

The powers of this goddess who is considered one of the most important Buddhist deities were invoked as a protection for us and to aid in both our personal healing and our abilities to help heal others.

The town of Dharamsala is the hub of all Tibetan activities outside of their ancestral homeland and at 5,000 feet in the foothills of the Himalayas it lies an area of outstanding natural beauty. Countless varieties of trees grow here in this area of immense bio-diversity and the occasional splash of bright yellow from an abundantly growing shrub intersperses every shade of green and the edge of the narrow road approaching this small but bustling community falls away to reveal deep tree lined gorges. Dharamsala, sited in India is full of international seekers of spirituality as well as the regular camera carrying tourist and is none the less a little Tibet.

Whether they are monks in their yellow and saffron colored robes or shopkeepers wearing traditional costume, the features of the residents declare that they are exiles from the Land of Snow, ousted from their homeland by the Chinese.

It was in such a setting that we entered this revered Lama's dwelling where we were greeted by two smiling monks and shown to a large outside terrace. There was a roof covering the area but two sides were open to the elements and the feeling of being suspended in space prevailed, as we became aware of the sheer drop for we were hundreds of feet above the valley floor. At eye level large black birds floated on the thermals and here with the sensation of being half way between heaven and earth we were served the traditional butter tea.

A large carpet covered most of the floor, woven in the predominantly bright blues and reds that seem to be favored and the pattern was a Tibetan design with many symbols. The two walls were decorated with hanging thankas of beautiful silks, either hand painted or embroidered with images of powerful deities and an ornate gilt-framed chair padded with a large cushion and with a footstool set in front of it was at end of this area and this was the only piece of furniture.

The monks stood to one side while we drank our tea and soaked in the beauty of our surrounding, then bowing to each of us as they retrieved our empty cups and with hand signals and smiles they requested us to seat ourselves on the carpet.

A hush fell over our chattering group as a small, elderly and portly gentleman clad in monks robes silently walked in and seated himself on the chair. His arrival was announced in no other way than his presence, but such was his aura it called for attention, we shuffled around from our positions looking out into the distance and faced him.

The Green Tara Ceremony commenced.

How could one fail to be touched by this momentous day? We understood no words of the ritual but it was steeped in ancient mystical tradition and spoken in the Tibetan dialect. The sound and the feel of the striking on the brass bowls by his attendants emitting a vibration that penetrated through your very being, a sound that you feel continues into eternity while background chanting from the monks who had been our attentive waiters accompanied all this.

We sat there immobile with our heads bowed, the blessed Kata scarves still hanging around our necks. We watched the symbolic lighting of candles, the throwing of rice and the sprinkling of water, all acts performed with a deep reverence, asking for the assistance of the deities and Green Tara in particular.

There was a timelessness to it all and the essence of the ceremony encompassed the whole group, it was so powerful that it felt as if it was seeping into our very souls.

A flight to Delhi the following day and a few hours shopping in the huge variety of stores this city has to offer all helped to ground me and I departed from this trip with a reluctance to bid farewell to my new found friends.

My head was still swimming as I boarded a plane heading for England, my Khata scarf was lovingly wrapped and placed in my hand luggage for safe keeping and as I gazed out at the clouds, my thoughts drifting aimlessly.

Without warning a voice in my head suddenly said

"You must give the scarf to Lyn"

Once more into my life came the voice that several years ago had dominated my life for weeks.

This voice was the same one that had rocked my life and sent me from my comfortable lifestyle onto a worldwide quest.

Who was Lyn? I didn't know anyone called Lyn. I didn't know who it was talking about. But strangely I didn't feel the least upset at being told I had to part with this recently acquired treasure and there was complete and unquestioning acceptance of this instruction.

Once in England I would have just a brief overnight stop before continuing on to Ireland.

My flight arrived in mid- afternoon where my husband met me and together we went to our hotel in central London.

It had been many hours and a time change since I had begun this journey from Delhi and I was feeling very weary and looking forward to a shower, a hair wash and a short sleep. Before I left on my trip we had made arrangements with my son who would be joining us for dinner that evening and I wanted to be alert enough to enjoy his company and catch up on all his news

As we drove into the City my husband was chattering away telling me of what he had been up to in the three weeks since we'd last been together, most of it was drifting past me. So far from the mountains and monks of the Himalayas, it was difficult trying to assimilate myself back into the London metropolis.

Then, like a bolt from the blue the word Lyn leapt out of his monologue. It brought me out of my reverie and he instantly had my attention.

"What was that you were saying? Tell me again" I insisted.

Apparently the previous day he had been out on the gallops watching one of our horses in training and he then patiently repeated what he had been telling me.

"Well", he began "I was with our trainer watching the horses and some other owners were there with us one of the ladies owns a horse that will be racing at Ascot next week, the same Meeting that one of ours is racing at she is a really nice lady; I expect you will meet her there and I am sure you will like her, her name is Caroline". He stopped at this point.

"Oops! Its not, I must remember it's CaroLYN. She's very particular about it". He continued talking and I now listened intently "While I was stood with her she turned to Micky (our trainer) and said "Micky! You've known me for ten years. Will you please stop calling me Caroline. I'm forever telling you its CaroLYN".

Instantly I knew that this was the person for whom the scarf was intended. The emphathis on this part of her name left me in no doubt.

This feeling grew as Barry went on with the story.

"I saw she had what appeared to be a bad back problem, for she had difficulty walking and was leaning heavily on her sister. Before long she need help to get back into the car and her sister then rejoined the rest of us.

We were standing watching the horses go through their paces and I asked her "Does Carolyn have a slipped disc?" and she repied "I wish it were that simple, she has cancer"

A voice within my head confirmed positively that this was the lady who was to be the recipient of the Khata scarf.

We arrived at the Hotel, checked in and got to our room where I immediately took a quick shower and then fell into bed.

I lay there and the thoughts running through my head were

'that's perfect, I know who the scarf is for, I'll be meeting her next week and give it to her then' it was a very satisfying feeling.

I closed my eyes and prepared for a couple of hours sleep, but it was not to be, for a dialogue then ensued between the voice and me.

VOICE. *She needs it now*

ME I'll give it to her next week. I want to sleep. I can't do anything about it now

VOICE. *Yes you can*

ME I can't. Its 4.30 pm Daniel is arriving to spend the evening with us in a short while. I leave again at 7.30am tomorrow morning and right now I need to go to sleep.

VOICE *Wake up. Get her address*

ME "I'm too tired

VOICE *Do it NOW*

It was impossible to ignore and I hauled myself out of the bed and went into the sitting room and I sleepily said to the husband

"Do me a favor. Please would you ring Micky and get Carolyn W's address. One look at my bleary eyes told him it was pointless to question why.

He simply said "Sure, go back to bed".

Thankfully I slipped once more back under the covers. I heard him make the call and walk back into the bedroom. He muttered something and I was aware that he had placed the written address on the bedside table.

Again.......

VOICE *Sit up.*

ME. Please let me sleep. I'll put the scarf in an envelope when I wake up and ask the Hotel reception to post it for me"

VOICE *Wake up, sit up and read the address*

It was so demanding there was no choice and reluctantly I obeyed the order and sat up. The address written on the piece of paper started with the words RAVEN COURT and then gave a town thirty miles outside the capital; beneath this Barry had written the telephone number.

The raven, the sacred messenger bird was playing his part. More confirmation that this was indeed the planned and right full owner of the precious Kata scarf.

VOICE. *Now phone her*

It was an order and by now I had accepted that there was no chance of a moments sleep until every act the voice demanded had been completed.

I dialed the number Carolyn answered the phone and my introduction went something like this...

"Hello Carolyn. My name is Wendy".

There was a need to keep it brief and to the point.

We've never met but you met my husband on Lambourn gallops the other day. I've just returned from India where I was fortunate enough to meet the Dalai Lama, I have a small silk scarf which he has handled and blessed and which I was also wearing during another powerful ceremony. I feel very strongly that it contains healing energies and I know it is meant for you. I don't know whether you are supposed to wear it, keep it in your pocket or put it under your pillow just follow your instinct and place it where ever it feels right for you, because all I know for certain is that this gift is definitely for you.

I'm staying overnight at the Connaught Hotel in London and I'm going to just put it in one of their envelopes and post it to you. It should arrive in a couple of days.

There was a short silence. Then I heard her say "Do you think you could take it into my office, I'll be there first thing in the morning".

By this time it was about five o'clock.

"Carolyn I'm so sorry" I said "But I just don't have the time"

Her next sentence left me dumbstruck

"My office is in the same street as the Connaught" she continued "It's in the basement below Strutts the estate agents."

I put the phone down, stepped out of the bed and walked the

few steps across to the bedroom window where I looked out. My hair stood on end and my skin prickled as I felt the unseen energies surround me. Directly opposite, right in my line of vision and less than 100 feet away was a window displaying photographs of properties for sale. The sign above the window read Strutt & Co. Estate Agents.

Within minutes the article in question was safely on her desk, I was back in bed with mission complete and immediately allowed to sink into a short but wonderful and restful sleep.

NB1 This trip triggered my desire to learn more of shamanism and on my return to England I searched the bookstores for anything I could find on this subject. It was later when I was browsing through these books that one particular item grabbed my attention. Here I found something very interesting; it was in the Shaman book in the Living Wisdom series and it showed a picture of three seated women

with shawls covering their heads and faces. The description beside it read. "Philippine women shamans with their faces covered as they prepare to go into trance".

This fueled some deep thinking and questioning. Prior to my meeting with John Perkins I knew less than nothing about shamanism, I knew nothing about journeying or trance states, and most certainly was unaware that women shaman in the Philippines covered their heads and faces.

What are the odds that I should place a shawl over a wall behind me as I began almost my first experience of what shamans call journeying?

How great are the odds that at the precise moment I slipped into trance the wind should lift that shawl and flip it completely over my head and face?

It was an amazing synchronicity that for me signaled other forces were at work.

Chapter 9

ALL THE NINES

The following day, I left London and returned to Ireland.

It was very difficult to settle back into a 'normal' life after the extraordinary events that had happened during the trip to India – in fact it was almost impossible. Each day, I looked out for a raven or the sight of any black bird but there was none. I took long solitary walks on the beach, seeing only the odd sandpiper which totally ignored me as it went about its business.

I relived the incredible events that had taken place during the trip through Ladakh. My head was filled with the memories of that epic journey and I spent most of the time during my chosen solitude recalling each day whilst it was still fresh in my mind. There was no one with whom I could share my experience; it was beyond rational understanding and I knew that if I told Barry he would either be concerned or else disparage and totally dismiss it. It did seem too strange to be true. Yet it had all happened.

Having just purchased a laptop, I made full use of this new tool and, as honestly as I could and without embellishment, recorded exactly what I had experienced. The empathy I had discovered with Shamanism had touched me deeply and I knew I had to delve further into these beliefs. Although I was half the world away from my newfound friends, the loneliness of the path I had been following for several years had vanished, partly because I already had a date in the near future when I knew I would meet up with many of them again.

On the Ladakh trip I had learned that Eve had already planned and organized an event entitled 'Gathering of the Shamans'. It was to be held at the Omega Institute in New York State and would take place over a weekend at the beginning of

September; she had been working on it for many months and her aim was to bring shamans from the Andes and the Amazon out of their homelands to the USA. Most of these indigenous people had never traveled beyond their village, but Eve was motivated by a personal experience on her first trip to the Andes three years previously: she had been very ill and a shaman had restored her health almost instantly, something that as a trained doctor and surgeon she knew was impossible using Western medicine. Now she was aiming to show as many people as possible how powerful these ancient shamanic healing rituals can be and also how speedily they produce beneficial results.

Not only was I determined to attend this weekend seminar but I was also planning to join John as part of a small group he was taking to Ecuador in October. This trip to South America would involve visiting and working with shamans, both in the Andes and also deep in the rainforest where we would spend five days staying with the Shuar people. Here we could observe the shaman of this head-hunting tribe at work.

Once more I was prepared to step into the unknown. Why was I doing it? What was it that was pushing me out of my comfort zone? There was no logical reason. I had a very enjoyable lifestyle, with the freedom to travel and stay in decent hotels if I so desired. Why did I need to go halfway round the world to spend time in the Amazon jungle? There were no answers, just an internal force driving me forward.

I swung between nervous excitement and trepidation, and all the while the little voice in my head was constantly saying, *You don't have to go. Staying at home would be so much easier.* But I knew I had to, for in spite of the fear, the powerful inner compulsion was urging me on.

However, there was to be another trip before either of these. Suddenly everything was moving: after all the years of constant searching, my life had a new momentum. I realized it had been a long nine years since that first spiritual explosion, and four and a half since the shape-shift into a snake in that suburban home. Now, after seeking and waiting for so long, events were happening very quickly.

One of the many subjects I had explored in my quest had been numerology. This science had fascinated me and I accepted there was a special power in certain arrangements of numbers. I guess this fact was somehow locked into the back of my head, for when Barry casually asked me where I would like to go for my birthday – probably expecting me to reply with the name of a favorite restaurant – my response to this matter-of-fact question surprised even me. It was the year 1999 and my birthday is the ninth day of the ninth month. With no thought at all and without a moment's hesitation, the words that came out of my mouth were, 'Machu Picchu!'

I was surprised at what I said, for it came out of nowhere. My husband looked a little shocked, but without questioning it he generously replied, 'Okay. I'll start making arrangements.'

The desire to go to this sacred place in Peru must have been seeded in my mind without my realizing it and have lain dormant for a very long time, but now that it was out in the open I became quite specific; the voice inside my head decreed that this wasn't to be a trip that simply *included* the anniversary of my birth, but rather I needed to actually be *on* the site of Machu Picchu *on* the ninth of the ninth, 1999.

I left all the chore of booking flights, hotels and travel arrangements to my partner; he was good at this and happy to take charge. Slowly over the years he had adjusted to the single-mindedness that I brought to my spiritual path, and maybe this slow but growing acceptance of the force that at times dominated my life persuaded him that there was more to life than the physical and the seen. Perhaps this was also part of his journey.

Since we were going as far as Peru, we mutually decided to extend our trip into Bolivia and also tied in a few days in Florida before I traveled up to New York for the Gathering of the

Shamans weekend at Rhinebeck. What a year this was turning out to be! I was right to follow my instincts, for yet another mystical experience was waiting for me, unknown and unsuspected, at the Inca citadel.

The majority of visitors to Machu Picchu start their trip at Cusco, which is the main town in Peru. From here, coaches leave by the dozen and deposit their passengers at a small rail station at the base of the mountain on which the remains of the ancient city of Machu Picchu are set. This part of the journey is an event in itself: a preparatory treat before arriving at 'Cloud City'. To get onto the platform is a bit of a nightmare, for hoards of tourists from a multitude of nations are funneled through a single gateway. It's all 'push and shove', and the most selfish part of each and every one of us gets exposed. But once on the train, having successfully claimed your allocated seat, a feeling of relief and calm descends.

As soon as the small steam engine with its many carriages starts puffing, a sense of expectation prevails. The train journey seems very much a part of the Machu Picchu experience and for me it equates to the half-mile walk to the pyramids at Giza or the aisle walk to the altar in a cathedral.

The rail track meanders around and around the base of the magnificent Peruvian mountains, following the curve of the river, which runs continually on the left-hand side. A sheer tree-covered expanse of rock stands vertically on the other side, only a distance of a few feet from the edge of the train. Mood-enhancing music comes from the internal speakers, relaying the true sounds of Peru: the lilting reed pipes and guitar. For an hour your ears are serenaded by the deeply evocative sounds of instruments at home in the landscape. They provide a balance and unity with the grandeur of the setting.

As the train draws to a halt at its destination, the occupants pour out and pass through an array of stalls selling an assortment of jewelry, crystals, clothes and locally made artifacts, before transferring to a fleet of small coaches. Snorting and blowing like an elderly dragon, a convoy of these vehicles – their engines in lowest gear – completes the final stages of the journey, zigzagging up the steep sides of Crystal Mountain to its very peak.

It is here, high above the valley, that the remains of the ancient city stand. Tier upon tier of stone walls stand in remarkable order, protected as they were for centuries under a jungle canopy. This enigmatic city remains an example of classic Inca architecture, displaying hundreds of precisely cut stone blocks and trapezoidal doorways. The sheer scale of the site is awesome, and the river some 1,300 feet below now appears like a mere ribbon. The recognition that this was a sacred place must certainly have been the reason the city was built in this location, for it is impossible to even begin considering the logistics of construction on such terrain.

Adjacent to the entrance into this ancient place is a small refreshment area and, adjoining this, a small hotel with a handful of rooms. It was here that we were staying for the night; it was the eighth of September and my birthday was the following day. After checking in, I immediately made my way into this most famous of places.

Once through the gateway, however, I looked with horror and felt quite sick! Due to increased accessibility, the popularity of this place had increased dramatically in the last few years and it was like watching ants crawling over a jam pot. There were so many tourists! Large groups milled around, and everyone was talking loudly and blocking the narrow paths. Those out for the day, dressed in shorts and tank-tops, sat on the walls quaffing canned drinks and eating snacks. People stood on the ancient stones posing for photos, while others viewed the complex through the lens of a video camera.

It is really none of my business how others view these sites. Why should it matter to me? Sadly it does. I understand that this is part of my learning process: I need to develop tolerance. But the attitude of some people is something I still struggle with. I feel deeply that Machu Picchu, along with the rest of the ancient and holy sites on our planet, deserves to be treated with respect.

I headed for the highest point, away from the crowds. Slowly I walked up and up, arriving at the point where the Inca trail stretches backwards for twenty miles before it finally reaches its destination. This ancient stone trail runs up, down and around the mountains, through valleys and across rivers. It's a pathway still in constant use, and for the fit and adventurous it is the perfect way to approach Machu Picchu. This was a journey I had considered, but after discovering that there are three high passes, one at around 14,000 feet, I reluctantly dropped the idea. Being now at the crone stage of my life, I have to accept that some things are physically beyond my capabilities.

At this high vantage point, I sat and surveyed all below me. What a view! The whole of this magnificent Lost City of the Incas was laid out before me, the 'ants' faded into insignificance when viewed from this height, and the power of the place pervaded all. For some time I sat in this spot, away from my fellow sightseers, absorbing the peaceful silence and enraptured by the sheer scale and grandeur of Machu Picchu.

Then, reluctantly getting to my feet, but knowing I would have the opportunity to return the following day, I slowly made my way down through the terraces, treading on step after step – on stones trodden by feet a million times over the centuries. By now the crowds had thinned out and most of the visitors had left, as the gates close at sundown and they needed to return to find room on the train. The hotel where I was staying clings to the edge of the mountain, and apart from the few rooms it contains, there is nowhere else close to stay. Deep down in the valley there are a few campsites, so only those planning on an overnight stay there and prepared for a long walk down the mountain side lingered behind. Everyone else had already taken advantage of the small coaches to return to the base of the mountain to connect with the last train back to Cusco, a facility that ceases to operate after 5.00pm The energy from the presence of these visitors was dissipating rapidly and there was already a tangible sense that the unseen cosmic rhythm that enfolds Machu Picchu was regaining its dominance. I walked out through the gates, one of the last to leave, thinking only of returning at first light when they were once again unlocked.

My alarm woke me the following morning. At its first buzz I was out of bed and full of anticipation; it was still dark, but as I quickly dressed, a hint of light came through the window and heralded the dawn of a new day. It was my birthday. The date was 9.9.1999 and my feelings were no different from those of a child excited by the expectation of prettily wrapped presents. But my gift would be the opportunity to have a few hours in near-solitude on the sacred site of Machu Picchu.

Barry had remained in bed, relieved that I hadn't asked him to accompany me at this early hour, so with a handful of others I made my way to the entrance and waited for the gate to be unlocked. It is easy to forget that this area is geographically a cloud forest, but the reminder was there in the form of a thick mist. Temperatures in this region drop rapidly at night and the morning mist is typical of the weather. The night was still reluctant to leave, and combined with the curtain of dampness, visibility was only about a hundred yards. I hoped it would clear before sunrise.

There was a strange stillness about the place. What little sound there might be was muffled, and as our little group of early-risers stepped inside, we all rapidly disappeared into the gloom. But we were needful of no other company and were watched only by the llamas that freely roam and graze these terraces.

Again I headed upwards. Although my legs were still aching from climbing so many steps the day before, without making any conscious decision this is the direction they took me. I reached a point where I paused. I had walked with my head down, simply focusing on the step ahead, performing a walking meditation. Now I turned and sat down.

The mist was thinning and it was a little lighter, although the surrounding mountains were still just darker shapes in the distance. Such is the size of this site and so numerous are the walls and small buildings that I could see nothing moving – no humans, no llamas – and no sound. I felt cocooned, as if I was inside an egg and the shell was a force of energy. For the moment, I felt that this place I was presently in was all there was. Then the egg grew larger and larger, the aura expanded, and I experienced a primordial connectedness with all life.

It was at this moment that I noticed I had a companion. I had neither seen nor heard him arrive, but sitting by my side was a small dog. He was right alongside me, seated as I was, facing outwards; as I glanced down at him, his head turned and he looked up at me.

He was a light brown color, with a white chest. His ears were not a matching pair; one was turned over, giving him a slightly quizzical look. Not a puppy but a young dog, he had a friendly demeanor.

We sat together for a few minutes. It was still quite cold so I got up and decided to walk some more. Without any bidding, the dog accompanied me, walking just a few feet away, stopping when I did and continuing when I chose to. The mist was now thinning quickly and one area in the sky was lighting up and starting to glow. It was apparent that the sun would soon herald the dawn of another day.

I scanned the area around me and spotted a position where I could observe the sunrise. The sun has risen over these mountains for millions of years. Today it was my birthday treat to participate in this most natural of ceremonies.

Again up the steps I climbed, the little dog leaping nimbly

alongside. As I reached a small plateau, I was hoping to be alone and was disappointed to find two men already there, one with a tripod and camera set up and ready, the other poised with his eye at his camera lens – both waiting to capture this moment. Approaching from the other side was another couple.

It would have been perfect to have had this spot to myself but there was no time to move elsewhere, so I sat down on a large stone, hoping at least that my companions would not start to chatter. The little dog made no attempt to seek out the friendship of the others, choosing to ignore them and position himself at my feet.

The sky took on a pink then a yellow glow as we awaited the sun. The light started to spread in the sky, even before the source of this light appeared over the mountain. Despite the immense distance between this great star and the earth, such was its power that the mist rapidly withdrew and the chill in the air vanished. I sat quietly composed, wrapped in the peaceful stillness.

The first brilliant rays appeared and I felt the light strike my forehead. I might just as well have been hit by a lightning bolt, such was my dramatic reaction. One moment I was sitting relaxed; the next I had leapt to my feet, arms outstretched, reaching out as energy poured into me. It all seemed to happen simultaneously. The next thing I knew, I was on my knees with my forehead on the ground, great shudders passing through me. Then I prostrated myself, lying cross-shaped on the ground. I remained in this position while waves of 'something' rippled through me, a force of an unseen power. I lay there until slowly they lessened and ebbed away, and then I started to quietly cry.

The action of leaping to my feet had been instant and automatic. Somehow there had been an immediate removal of all egotistic feelings; all inhibitions were swept away. The projected image of a reserved lady of middle years fell away and I succumbed wholly to a split between consciousness and body.

Some active force beyond human understanding had been triggered. But now I was back to my normal level of understanding and the more familiar feeling of embarrassment took its place. I scrambled to my feet, fumbling for tissues to wipe my face and blow my nose. Trying to keep my head down, I turned and hurriedly looked for an exit from this area.

Little Dog, who was still by my side, led the way; I followed him out between two pillars, then down the steps, as he walked just one step in front of me. We started to descend, and as we did so, I saw two women in single file with a man close behind, making their way up.

It requires lungfuls of air to climb on these mountains at this altitude; only children and the super fit can climb and talk at the same time. These people were not young and so were reserving all their energy for the physical effort. In no way were they presenting an aggressive image. But to my surprise, Little Dog suddenly stopped, stared straight at them and let out a menacing growl.

Startled, they stopped and looked up at him. He repeated it, this time more loudly. Then, staring at them, he curled back his upper lip and bared his teeth, all the while continuing his deep-throated growl. They recoiled in horror. The image the dog projected transformed him; this sweet little creature had become a ferocious beast. His hackles went up, standing like porcupine bristles. The three visitors froze as the dog maintained his pose.

Then I heard a man's voice call out from behind me, from the plateau I had just left. With some authority he said, 'Move right over to one side and then stand still!' Then he gave an order to the three people: 'He's a guardian dog. Let him and the lady pass.'

The group was transfixed in their fear; very cautiously they followed his orders. Once they had moved sufficiently, Little Dog seemed appeased; his hairy coat started to flatten but he was slightly stiff-legged as he walked past. He glanced over his back as if checking that I had safely passed them; then, assuming his earlier attitude, he bounced on down the steps, keeping pace with me.

We continued wandering around for about another hour. As I walked across one area, I suddenly saw Barry standing in front of me with his camera held up to his eye. He had just taken a photo of us. It was a picture that I later had framed: me in my jaguar print jacket with the dog by my side, as the pair of us walked out of the mist. It stood on a chest in my home in England for ten years – just a nice picture, I thought, all the time completely unaware that it was a link to much more. Ten years later, it would be revealed how it connected in a powerful and extraordinary way to the South American, Mayan god Kukulkan, but that was a long way off in the future.

The dog ignored all of Barry's attempts to pat him and for another couple of hours the three of us walked the ancient site, the little dog never more than a couple of yards from my side. Who led whom I don't know; we simply sojourned together.

By now the site was starting to fill. The coaches had commenced their repetitive trip up the mountainside. Little Dog was oblivious to everyone. Several times people stopped to speak to him and tried to give him a pat; he showed no further aggression, just total indifference.

He had assumed the role of my chaperone and this he did all the way back to the hotel lobby. There he turned. I watched from a window for a while and saw him weaving his way in and out of the crowds that milled around the entrance. Then he vanished.

Barry and I went to the dining room and enjoyed my birthday breakfast together. As we were sitting there, he was observant enough to notice something I had failed to see.

'Where's your piece of string?' he asked.

I glanced down at my finger: the red thread which had been tied around my ring finger by the shaman in Ladakh and which had been there yesterday was missing. It was certainly on my finger the previous day, as it had been for over three months.

Now, on this auspicious day in this very sacred place and in the company of a new guardian, this protective symbol had vanished of its own accord.

Before joining our transport back to Cusco, I returned to the site. Taking a few slices of meat from the breakfast buffet, I went in search of the little dog, but I never saw him again.

The unusual behavior of this animal puzzled me. Pausing on the return journey to Cusco, I shared a conversation with an elderly Peruvian guide and asked him what he knew of any dogs that frequented the ancient site. He looked at me thoughtfully, then said, 'Ah, the temple guardian. Occasionally one of these dogs will appear and attach themselves to one they consider special. They will remain with them while they are in the Sacred Place.' Then he gave an enigmatic smile and walked away.

A few days later I bought a book called *The Awakening of the Puma*, translated from Spanish; it offers evidence of archeoastronomy in the Andes. There were also chapters on ancient initiation rites. It was a picture on page 153 that caught my eye: a re-enactment of one of these ancient rituals. The photograph showed a woman at Machu Picchu. But what truly amazed me was that she was standing in the same position as I had been when I experienced that mysterious event. The photo showed the first rays of the morning sun striking her forehead. The caption underneath read, 'The priestess receives the Sun's light on her forehead. The initiation directly given by our planet, Pachamama, and the Creator god, Wiracocha, has begun.'

I hold a collection of incredible personal experiences, the bestowing of which continually reminds me how blessed and honored I am. Many of these experiences have taken me into the spiritual sphere and have, on occasion, left me struggling with the feeling that I am a little mad. However, I hold on to a quote attributed to Socrates: 'The greatest blessing comes to us on the way to madness.'

Before the last days of September 1999 had expired, I was at the Omega Institute in Rhinebeck, New York, attending the first assembly of the 'Gathering of the Shamans' held by the Dream Change Coalition. Eve Bruce, in spite of her heavy workload as a plastic surgeon, had managed to draw shamans from many parts of the world to this point in upstate New York. Many of these shamans had never been far from their villages before, never sat in a car or a plane, or seen the ocean. After coming out of the mountains or from deep in the jungle, they were housed for a short period of rest and preparation with families connected to the organization.

I later learned that one of the shamans, who had never seen the ocean before, was by chance taken to the beach on the night of the full moon. He looked at the reflection of the moon on the water and remarked, 'Ah! Now I see what has always been a powerful symbol for us. This is called the Shaman's Path.' On hearing about this, the hair on my head stood up, for this was the symbol I had been given as my first power tool when I was in the far-distant Hemis monastery in Ladakh four months before.

The logistics involved in the organization of this event must have been horrendous, but Eve Bruce, a remarkable woman, had achieved it, thereby bringing indigenous wisdom not only to countless people in North America but also to those, like me, who had come from other countries. Several of us who had met on the trip to India were here reveling in this weekend event and I was very happy to be back amongst like-minded people.

On the Friday evening at the start of this gathering, John had introduced the various shamans and shared a little of their history. Then, over the course of the weekend, they were all busy giving individual healings. The majority of people attending were hoping to have a healing and the list was long. Because I was booked to take a trip to the territory of the Shuar in just a few weeks, I refrained from adding my name, but I was very drawn to a Shuar shaman named Daniel and hoped he would be one we would be seeing again on the forthcoming trip. Some of these shamans were happy for us to watch them at work as long as the patient was agreeable, which was a fascinating experience and at first seemed very different from the way the Tibetan shamans worked.

I walked around the campus, looking and listening, and sat in on many healings. I noted that there was one shaman, a Brazilian named Ipupiara Makunaiman who was, assisted by his wife, a beautiful Peruvian lady named Cleicha Toscano, also a healer and they asked that each person bring three red carnations with them as they presented themselves for a healing. This triggered my memory of the key-bending occurrence that had happened over nine years before, when I had shared with my mother the synchronistic carnation story.

Without mentioning why I was enquiring, I found the opportunity to ask the shaman why he was requesting carnations. He looked at me and briefly answered, 'Because it is the most powerful flower.' His expression suggested it was an unnecessary question, for surely everyone knows that!

On the Sunday, the final morning of the weekend event, over three hundred of us were sitting in the main hall as one of the shamans from Ecuador was due to speak. It turned out to be the shaman to whom I felt so drawn: Daniel Wachapa, a member of the Shuar tribe that still resided deep in the Amazon rainforest. Apart from hunting forays, when the men go trekking for several days from their home, this was his first time away from his village, which lies in a remote and barely accessible area. He was the powerful shaman and healer whom I had first seen on the Friday evening at the opening ceremony, when all the shamans participating in this unique gathering had been seated on the stage and John Perkins had introduced each of them to the attendees.

The aura and energy surrounding this man drew me like a magnet and I dearly hoped I would have the opportunity to meet him in the following month. This was a distinct possibility, for I was booked to go on a Dream Change trip to South America with John Perkins and Dr Eve Bruce as facilitators – a journey that would take us not only into the mountains of the Andes but also deep into the jungle of Daniel's country.

Janet and I had found ourselves good seats and listened attentively as John told his own story: how he had been in the Peace Corps and spent nearly five years living with the Shuar; after completing his three-year compulsory duty, he had voluntarily stayed on for an extra two years, feeling the need to learn from these people how to live a sustainable lifestyle. His account of how he had originally set out to 'convert' these people to a Western way of living – and the shift he made in recognizing that we are the ones who need to change – is fascinating. These were the people whose daily lives had inspired him and I eagerly waited to hear Daniel talk.

This small but immensely strong man moved to the front of the stage. These days, many of his people speak a little Spanish and wear shorts and T-shirts, but he was wearing the traditional Shuar clothing, complete with feathered headdress. An interpreter moved alongside him and he started to speak.

He had uttered no more that a couple of sentences, and the translating had not yet commenced, when a feeling of panic swept over me. It came in very fast and I felt myself getting very emotional. I needed Eve. I needed to be with Eve, *now*.

As well as being a talented plastic surgeon with a busy practice and a member of several boards, Eve Bruce was a hands-on mother and grandmother and had also set up the website for the Dream Change Coalition and was its webmaster. The trip to India was the first and only time so far that our paths had crossed. She had been so busy coordinating this weekend's event that we had not had a chance to talk at length, and due to the demands on her time over the past couple of days we had done no more than exchange hugs. Yet now I suddenly and desperately needed to be with her.

I was seated towards the back of the hall. Looking around and over my shoulder, I scanned the room for her. She wasn't there. The feeling of anxiety had come out of nowhere: a moment before, I had been sitting looking forward to the talk, but now my overwhelming priority was to find Eve. I got to my feet, and making my excuses, passed along the row of seats to the aisle, then fled out of the door and from the hall.

Tears started to flow down my face and I started to run. Where I was going, I don't know – I just started running down the path. The campus was deserted; everyone was in the hall and there was no one in sight. Then suddenly, right in front of me, there she was! A lone figure wrapped in a stunning red cape came strolling towards me.

'Eve!' I cried, and threw myself onto her.

We sat on a nearby bench in the autumn sunshine and talked. I truly can't remember what we spoke about, but such is her understanding that, very quickly, my emotional outburst subsided, leaving me wondering what it had all been about. Eve had work to do, so we walked back along the path and returned to the hall. As we went through the doors we were met by the resounding applause for Daniel.

Dr Bruce went in one direction and I rejoined my friends. I had missed all of Daniel's talk and was anxious to hear what he had said. Janet, my companion from the Ladakh trip, started to tell me, but first she said this: 'Just before you left so suddenly, the strangest thing happened. I was sitting there with my eyes closed, meditating, as Daniel started talking in his native language, and I felt something move across my feet. For all the world, it was as if a huge snake was passing across me on its way to you! I felt my skirt move as it passed by. The sensation was so real. Interestingly, his talk then focused on the giant anaconda.'

Janet has her feet firmly on the ground and is not given to fanciful talk, so what she said sounded very strange. But since I had neither seen nor felt anything and could offer nothing in the way of an explanation, we left it as a mystery.

I had just a few weeks to ponder on the bizarre events that were touching my life before I was on yet another airplane, en route to Quito and another adventure.

Chapter 10

AYAHUASCA – THE SACRED VINE

On this, my first trip to Ecuador, there was just a handful of participants venturing into the unknown. We were a small group being led by John Perkins, with Eve coming along to assist him. We were off to first visit shamans in the higher regions of this country before heading deep into the jungle to stay for five days in the village of Miazal.

Because of the extraordinary events that had occurred during my time with the shamans in Ladakh, I was feeling somewhat apprehensive leading up to the start of this trip, but there was no turning back and once I was at the airport and embarked on the six-hour flight, the hours passed swiftly, as though I was a stick being swept along a fast-flowing river.

At Quito we were met by John's friend and compadre, Juan Gabriel; this was a man who had been born and lived all of his life in many different areas of Ecuador and had shared many adventures with John. He would be accompanying and guiding us throughout our journey in his country, a place we soon realized he loved deeply.

After a brief overnight stay, we were up early; loaded into a small minibus, we set off for an area high in the Andes. We were heading to the community of Ortovalo, where our first port of call would be at the home of the Tamayo family. Three renowned shamans, all male, reside here in these snow-capped mountains. The father, Don Esteban, and his two sons, Jose and Jorge, live with their families in a group of small single-story, whitewashed buildings; each of these dwellings appeared to consist of only two rooms and reminded me very much in size and shape of traditional Irish houses.

The setting of these homes was breathtaking, for they were surrounded by three volcanic mountains. The peaks of Mohanda, Imbabura and Cotacachi dominate the landscape and are one of the sources from which these men draw the power to heal. The methods the shamans use are dramatic and effective, and a tangible energy is felt when merely watching them at work, for they draw on and use the spiritual power embodied in the elements that are so much a part of their daily lives; they invoke them and use them in their healing practice.

The shamans start with the cleansing of the patient and for this purpose *trago* (the local brew) is used in a very dramatic way. The ill person stands nude in front of them, but the alcohol is not supplied for gently wiping the body – far from it. Instead the shamans take a lighted candle and, by blowing a mouthful of this powerful brew through the flames, engulf the patient in a fireball. The shamans transform themselves into volcanoes – they shape-shift – and in so doing, the power of the flames becomes a cleansing agent.

The Tamayos also incorporate fresh spring water into the healing process and use treasured, sacred stones that have been passed down through the generations. A vigorous beating of the patient with stems from special plants is also part of this proven ritual.

Such is their success that their reputation has spread to many parts of the world. Nowadays, added to the patient line of villagers who daily wait for attention are individuals who have come a long way by plane in search of a cure.

The work these holy men do is fascinating and far removed from our Western 'pop a pill' culture. I was not sure what I was expecting. Although I kept an open mind, watched everything closely and was eager to learn, I still felt rather detached. I had a healing with them: I was engulfed in flames and beaten with the healing plants. But maybe I was expecting too much, for I still felt I was an observer rather than a participant.

Over the next couple of days we visited the sacred waterfalls and the home of another shaman, a woman who could reveal the cause of an illness by lighting a candle and 'reading' what the flame told her as it waved and flickered. As we traveled I was struck by the stunning beauty of this country; it is a land of majestic snow-capped mountains and deep valleys, inhabited by colorfully costumed people who are friendly and generous. I was interested in it all and eager to learn all I could about Shamanism; I was always the last one to leave each place we visited, remaining until the final moment before departing. But in a strange way, the experience wasn't resonating.

For some reason, I seemed to be focusing on the second half of the trip. Continually I was looking forward to the time when we would be deep in the jungle; in spite of the butterflies in my stomach signaling a degree of trepidation, I was almost looking forward to it and trying to speed up this initial part of the journey. At the same time, there was a constant voice in my head questioning what on earth I was doing here; there was no simple answer – just the 'knowing' that I had to do it.

Our five days in the mountains of Ecuador were soon over and we were back waiting in Quito airport for the small airplane that would take us into the jungle. Not very long ago the only access to Miazal was a nine-hour journey by Land Rover along a rough track, but now a small clearing has been made in the jungle, just big enough to enable a small light aircraft to safely land and take off (providing that the weather is clear; so often, the area is shrouded in mists). Carrying just a very small bag each, we finally boarded the plane, and after almost an hour's journey when all we could see were treetops, we bumped down into a clearing in the forest. After a further ride in a shallow dugout canoe, we reached our destination.

This was another excursion into a magical world, for here a part of our planet remains relatively untouched by the fingers of the Western world. In this very exclusive place dwells a diminishing group of people who still hold values and beliefs that were long ago dismissed by our culture. Who has it right? When you boil it down, all any of us need or want is to be loved and to be happy, and for the most part these people certainly are both. The constant query that John claims they throw at every group he takes in is, 'Why is everyone so unhappy?'

These people live in a closeness and harmony with nature that we, in our air-conditioned buildings and with our focus on consumerism, have long ago lost. Their lives are in balance; heart attacks and malignant cancerous growths simply do not occur in their society. Admittedly they have a mortality rate higher than we would desire, but this they find acceptable, for it maintains community sustainability.

It was during my stay with this community that I first heard of and partook of the substance known as *ayahuasca*. It is called by many names, including the Vine of the Soul, the Sacred Vine and the Teacher Plant. Ayahuasca is a psychotropic plant that enables the user to unite with all aspects of the natural world – to merge with the entire cosmos. It is offered by the shaman, who has prepared the foul-tasting liquid by pounding and boiling the bark, and then adding other plants in a combination known only to him. It is this magical mix of three plants from a choice of about 80,000 that gives the drug its potency. The information regarding the harvesting, preparation and value of this specific mix is deeply rooted in native mythology, and the claim is made that it was given directly to the Shuar by the gods.

Ingestion of this plant will induce a trance-like state in which one 'journeys'; it frees the soul to wander, to travel far and wide, and permits its owner to communicate with his or her ancestors. It is not a recreational drink and those who take it for frivolous purposes do so at their peril. There is a need to approach the taking of this vine with a certain reverence: to prepare by fasting and focusing the mind on what one wishes to learn. It is a powerful substance and not to be indulged in lightly. Once it has been taken, the physical body performs its own cleansing and will begin a purging shortly after the liquid is swallowed.

I was delighted to see that Daniel Watchapa had traveled the many miles from his own village to prepare the ayahuasca and to conduct the ceremony. The brief glance I had had of him in Omega had been enough to trigger what I felt was a deep connection with him; there had certainly been no meeting with him in this lifetime, but over the past few years the theory of reincarnation, which I had totally dismissed when I first came across it, had slowly festered in my mind. Recently I had come to accept the truth of this idea and the more I questioned it, the more I came to believe it.

Due to Daniel's presence, I felt comfortable and very reassured that all would go well on this night, for the preparation of the ayahuasca draught is a process requiring much knowledge and skill. It is extremely important for the practitioner to use precise quantities not only of the vine itself but also of the accompanying plants.

The round house, the communal place where we gathered when staying at our camp deep in the Ecuadorian rainforest, was an open-sided structure with a plant roof. A few hammocks hung from the trunks supporting the ceiling, there were benches on three sides, and in the evenings a fire would burn on the dirt floor in the center. However, on the night of the ayahuasca taking, there is no fire and none of the small paraffin lamps are lit. One of the physical peculiarities that ayahuasca produces is night vision – the user can see quite clearly on the darkest night – but it also produces an acute sensitivity to light.

As a safety precaution, each person partaking of the vine is given a guardian; one of the other trip participants offers themselves just for that evening as a helper, and the only light used is that of the partner's small torch. The guardian's task is to keep as close as a shadow to his or her companion until the full effects of the ayahuasca have passed and the 'journeying' has ceased.

For twenty-four hours before the event, I had fasted. I had hiked to the sacred waterfalls, immersing myself in the ice-cold water that runs from the snow-covered mountain all the way down to this river in the valley, and I had spent time in solitude and meditation. Now, in the soft gloom of the evening, I swallowed my measure of this magic potion and sat back on a bench with my partner beside me. The apprehension that endured during the day had passed, for now there was no going back; the deed was done. I sat still in the increasing darkness, listening to the sounds of the forest and waiting for the inevitable purging to begin – one aspect of the experience that we had been warned would start rapidly.

Although I was resting my back against the planking that provided a half-wall around part of the room, I had a distinct feeling that someone was standing behind me.

The intensity of the feeling increased and I felt a huge weight on my shoulders. Desperately I tried to keep my thoughts focused on the immediate, the 'now', and on the journeying that would soon commence. But amazingly, cutting into this moment in this most unlikely of places and settings, I became aware of a Tibetan deity. He was looming behind and over me; I felt the power of him encompassing me.

Then I started to yawn. The yawns became larger and deeper. I felt my mouth stretching to extremes. In my mind's eye I could 'see' the same deity that had first presented its image on the tanka hanging on the wall of the Tashi Delek Hotel in Gangtok. I had been aware of his presence in Ladakh. It was this same god that now invaded and engulfed my body as I sat deep in the Amazon rainforest. There was no mistaking the red face with three eyes, the fanged teeth and the band of small skulls around his head. The power and force of his energy was beginning to envelop my body.

At that moment John moved in front of me. 'Wendy, how are

you doing? Maybe you should take a walk outside.'

I was unable to answer. I stood to move but my legs buckled, and John and my partner helped me to a convenient log a few feet outside the round room. John has spent many years living and training with both the Shuar shamans and the Yatchak Birdmen who live in the high Andes; he has undergone many initiations with shamans from different countries and is a man with a unique perception and sensitivity.

'What was happening?' he asked me.

'A Tibetan deity,' was the most I could respond. But as I spoke, I realized it was clearing; the form of 'something else' that had surrounded me and almost engulfed me only seconds before was gone. The powerful energy had backed off and vanished.

'It's gone,' I said.

'Daniel the shaman is going to start the healings,' John said. 'Go back in if you're ready for one.'

I felt fine, quite normal, and as I stood up to re-enter the room I realized I was standing and walking without a problem. The huge weight that had seemed to sit on me, and the jelly-like sensation in my legs, had vanished. I went back into the round house that night and had my healing.

During this healing, the interpreter relayed a remarkable message to me: 'The shaman says, "You are a great warrior!"' I had no idea why he said this and I tucked the statement away into the recesses of my memory.

Right now, my physical body began to purge as the ayahuasca became effective; this is a process that the shamans believe is necessary, as the vine has the power to remove the destructive remnants of bad experiences from the past, memories of which are trapped in the subconscious mind. These remnants prevent us experiencing the more subtle levels of reality and so this preparatory discomfort has to be endured before the visions begin.

Finally, I felt as if the physical cleansing had come to an end, and with my partner supporting me, we went to our sleeping area. I lay down, put my head on the pillow and pulled the thin cover up and over me. The moment I closed my eyes I saw several tall buildings on my right-hand side, but I was about a hundred feet off the ground, flying and passing quite close to some windows. I seemed to be on a course that would take me on a circular route around the buildings, but also going ever upwards.

This vision lasted only moments; then I found myself looking through a glass wall at many, many snakes. The vision seemed to last an eternity. It went on and on, but suddenly the glass wall vanished and I was inside with the snakes, right amongst them. There were hundreds of them – all very active, moving and writhing around.

Next, the snakes changed shape and became of every type and color imaginable: large and small, they were hanging from trees, swimming in pools, wriggling over each other in large pits... but every one of them was ignoring me. I kept trying to communicate with them, but a silent message always came back: they were waiting for the giant anaconda to arrive. She was the one who would talk to me. I felt no fear, just a feeling of frustration at being ignored. But there was also an awareness that the snake for whom we were all waiting was a large and powerful being.

Suddenly the scene vanished and there was not a snake in sight. Now, in a condition far removed from a dream state, I found myself walking along a narrow jungle track. There was nothing dreamlike about this experience. It was *reality*.

The sun was filtering down through the tall trees, and everything was very beautiful and peaceful. I could feel the motions of my body as I walked in a relaxed, gentle way. I had gone only a very short way when I stopped and looked at something lying out on the path in front of me.

There, as if set out with perfection, was a shed snakeskin. It was huge. It was also perfect, with not a blemish or tear on it, and it filled the width of the single-file path and stretched about twenty feet ahead. In total awe I stood and gazed at it, then instantly the whole scene vanished and I found myself back in my bed in the cabin, in the darkness of the Amazon night. I was aware of my partner lying in the bed a few feet away and heard her voice asking if there was anything I needed.

I managed to say 'No, thank you', but wished to say no more, for the spell was broken. I desperately wanted to return in search of the anaconda, but this was denied me. Instead, as my ayahuasca-induced journey continued, I found myself facing a huge male gorilla; before I had time to think, his mouth had opened wide and I was swallowed whole.

Not in a million years was this a pre-suggested idea. The color and detail I observed was astounding as I whizzed at high speed down through the animal's esophagus. Somehow I knew exactly where I was as I sped through this round channel, a tunnel that twisted and turned, with a colorful lining of veins and blood vessels – mind-blowing in its incredible beauty.[1]

Then the Sacred Vine caused another shift and once more my level of consciousness lifted and altered. Again I was aware that I was back in bed in the cabin in the rainforest of Ecuador. I knew exactly where I was, but now the experience became difficult, for suddenly the positions were reversed: this time the gorilla was inside me.

I could feel him and see him down in the pit of my stomach. He was standing upright with his arms held high above his head, and in his hands he balanced a great boulder. Slowly and with a determined effort, he pushed this boulder up through me. I could feel it physically rising and moving towards my throat and I knew that once it got there, I would perform a projectile vomit.

The rock got to the point of my throat; then the gorilla could hold it no longer and he sank back down. Once more he repeated this process, slowly moving the huge boulder upwards. And again, just as it was almost ready to shoot out of my throat, the gorilla slipped back down again, still holding his burden.

A third time he started. Like a weightlifter with a huge powerful chest and bulging arm muscles, his determination was palpable. Little by little, with the boulder above him, he once more progressed on his upward journey. I could feel it and witness it but was incapable of either stopping or assisting the process.

Now I wanted the boulder out of me and was willing the gorilla to succeed. I felt him getting closer and closer to the top and once more he almost made it; the huge stone was on the brink, before the gorilla's strength faded and he failed yet again. At this point I saw he was exhausted; his power and strength were gone and I knew he could try no more.[2]

The vision faded and I realized my journey was over. I turned in my bed and fell into a dreamless sleep.

When I woke it was daylight; the morning had arrived. But as I lay there, I recalled everything I had witnessed in my ayahuasca journey. It all remained – clear and bright.

Before Daniel left on his long trek back through the jungle to his own village, we were invited to share our visions of the previous night with him. I listened as each of my companions shared the events of their night. Through an interpreter it was a difficult process, but the shaman did his best to give an interpretation of people's visions. He listened patiently to my tale, first of the snakes, then of the snakeskin and finally the gorilla; he sat quietly, all the while looking at me deeply but saying nothing at all. Then, when I had finished, his one comment was: 'She is a great warrior. She has much *arutam*.'

That was it. I was left to work it out for myself.

Two days later, our small plane arrived to take us back to civilization. It was then that we learned that one of the volcanoes had erupted and we would be unable to return to Quito. Our flight to an alternative airfield took us quite close to the still-active volcano and we witnessed the flames and ash shooting from the top. As I saw it, I wondered if my ayahuasca trip had been associated with these natural phenomena. Had the gorilla inside me been a warning of what was happening to the land around me? Maybe. Or was it, as I later came to accept, that there were also psychological and emotional blockages within me that needed to be removed in order for me to progress?

Whatever the reason, this was a journey that I was happy to have taken. The whole trip, but especially the partaking of the sacred potion of ayahuasca, had had such a profound effect on me that I knew I had to come back to Miazal.

I returned to England, and the following period was a time of consolidation and grounding. I knew my desire to learn more of Shamanism would not fade and that my continuing quest into the metaphysical world would be an ongoing journey. Having paid a deposit for a further trip with John to Ecuador which would take place the following year, in March 2000, my search continued. It was continually rewarded in many diverse and fascinating ways. Although I could often make no sense or find a reason for these events, they reinforced my beliefs and rewarded my efforts.

During this time I attended a group healing session in my hometown of Winchester with a man called Matthew Manning, a well-known British healer whose book I had enjoyed reading. Matthew was, I believe, one of the first to promote group sessions as an effective aid to healing and this is how he worked that particular day in Winchester Town Hall.

There were over forty participants present. We sat on chairs in a closed circle, holding hands, and were asked to visualize positive energy passing around the circle, touching every one of us. Matthew remained outside of the circle and stood behind each of us in turn for about one minute with his hands on our shoulders.

Before he commenced, he had explained that the session would be carried out in silence apart from the playing of soothing music. He suggested we keep our eyes closed, and simply relax and visualize beautiful colors. It was a restful and pleasant atmosphere, and I sat there feeling very calm and peaceful. The 'mood music' Matthew had chosen was that of gentle waves breaking on the seashore, interspersed with the cry of seabirds.

I sat waiting for the pictures to form, but I couldn't visualize anything. Usually I can have a scenario going on in my head even without closing my eyes; it has always been easy to form images in my mind. But right now, there was *nothing*. There was no sea, no sand and no birds. I could hear the sound of the waves continually breaking, but all I could see was a grey open space: a large barren field.

It was all very odd, and worse than that, there was no color – it was all in very subtle shades of black and white. I tried and tried but I could find no color, whilst all the time in my head I kept hearing the words 'Ten, ten o'clock, ten...' Much as I tried to produce some color, it was impossible. For some reason, I was unable to and was stuck with a sepia-tone field for almost the entire healing session. Then suddenly in the middle of the field – without any change in the music – there appeared a red poppy. Then another came and another. Quite dramatically the monochrome picture, moment by moment, became a meadow full of brilliant, scarlet, waving poppies. As it did so, the voice continually repeating the word 'ten' faded away.

The healing session finished and I drove home trying to puzzle out what had been going on in my head during that meditative state. I had no explanation, so just accepted it and left it filed away in my memory.

The following evening, after a day out, I returned home late and went into the kitchen. Whilst I was waiting for the kettle to boil, I glanced at the clock: it was nearly ten o'clock so I turned on the television and prepared to view the *Ten O'Clock News* program. The image on my color TV came on, but the picture that appeared was in black and white. What's more, it was just a field – a barren grey field. Then, as I watched transfixed, a red poppy appeared in the middle of this picture, then another and another. The screen changed very gradually and the monochrome picture became a meadow full of brilliant, scarlet, waving poppies. The scene was the final moments of the last episode of a comedy series set in the First World War, called *Blackadder Goes Forth*.

I have yet to be enlightened about the meaning of this 'coincidence', but the following day I began recording it while sitting on a non-stop train to London. Scribbling away in my exercise book, I happened to glance up at one point. We were passing through a station and the station clock read 10.10pm. The messages are around us every day in many diverse ways. The timing is immaculate.

There was to be another synchronicity the following month, reassuring me that someone was keeping watch over me – a thought that provides great comfort. This episode revolved around one of the great loves of my life.

Since I was a child, horses have held a special place in my heart. Many years ago I bought a foal, and he was to remain with me for nearly twenty-six years. The first time we met, he was only six months old and had just been weaned; he stood there with his long legs out of proportion to his body, but nevertheless so beautiful that when he turned his head and looked at me, I fell hopelessly in love.

Daily I watched him grow, and over the years he developed into a very handsome horse, with a nature that matched his looks: he was kind and courageous. The stable that was his home was in line with my kitchen window. I never ceased to find joy at the sight of his long white face looking expectantly at the house.

We had matured together, Peron and I. There was compatibility in the way his mane and tail, so black in his youth, became quite white with age, while my grey hairs began to outnumber the brown.

At the age of twenty-four he was still sprightly and being ridden out regularly. Then he became ill, very ill. I feared the end of his life was near as the vet was not hopeful, but to everyone's surprise he fully recovered. Six months later he needed an operation. Because of his age, the risk with the anesthetic and the complicated operation itself, the veterinary surgeon was not hopeful of success. But without the operation he would have had no quality of life, so in spite of the large cost I knew I had no choice. Peron deserved the chance. It was touch and go, but he fought this battle and slowly recovered.

However, the next thing that hit him was a virus, which brought him once again to death's door. It was at this stage that I renamed him 'Lazarus' – he had come back from the dead so many times. I even wrote to the veterinary surgery and suggested they change the name on his record card.

A while later, I was away on holiday when I had a phone call from his carer to say that my beloved horse had died. Even my belief that life for every living thing continues and that there is no end, only a shape-shift into another form, seemed of little help at this time. The realization that I would never, after so many years, see his gorgeous white face again was very painful.

I was still very upset when, later that day, I was out driving to a destination through an unfamiliar area, my thoughts still with the loss of my horse. My eyes were drawn to glance sideways as I passed a small white building, and after continuing a few hundred yards further on up the road, I had a compelling urge to go back. The feeling swept over me and was so strong that it was impossible to ignore. It seemed I had no choice but to slow down, turn the car around and drive back.

When I pulled up outside, I saw that the building was a Catholic church. I parked the car, went to the door, found it was unlocked and opened it. I walked in wondering what I was doing. My 'tidings of great joy' were immediate. Right in front of me was a large statue of a man and written in bold print underneath were the words 'St Lazarus'.

Saint Lazarus is not one of the most popular icons, and holy statues are usually recognized by their symbol; rarely do they carry the name of the subject. I smile now when I hear the statement 'There's only one life and this is it!' because I remain convinced that not only humans but all animals have a spirit that is eternal. My grief dissolved instantly that day, for I have no doubt that it was a message from Peron and that one day we shall meet again.

I had by now become computer literate and this new technology eased the isolation I had been feeling in my spiritual search up to this point. Now I had the opportunity to access books and information, discover the availability of workshops and keep easily in touch with the like-minded friends I was making on my journeys. My life was running smoothly and all the while I was looking forward to my return trip to Ecuador.

Then a strange thing happened: I began to have a series of dreams that were close to nightmares. They started about three weeks before the departure date of the planned trip and were totally unexpected. There was nothing in my daily life that might have triggered them, but they were vivid and strong, and each morning I would wake up with an instant and total recall.

Each dream was almost identical and I knew without doubt that the picture I was seeing was somewhere in the Ecuadorian jungle – somewhere near Miazal. It was not a scene I had tucked away in my mind from the last visit, but I knew for certain that this was the location.

Every night in this vision I would be standing in the same spot on the bank of a fast-flowing river. The water was flowing from left to right and the piece of land where I stood seemed to project into the river; the curve of the stream was flowing faster and more turbulently on the opposite side, as it swung around a sharp and slightly narrowed bend. I noticed that the jungle on the opposite bank was thick with many tall trees, whilst I seemed to be in a small clearing. I was always aware of one or two local children around me and a wooden thatched dwelling to my left.

Each night the dream would be the same: I would see a dugout canoe (the main form of transport for the Shuar) come speeding into view, but as it traversed the corner it suddenly tipped, throwing the occupants into the dark water. This scene filled my thoughts throughout the day until gradually I accepted that I was being given a warning.

I desperately wanted to go on the trip to Ecuador. On my first visit I had thoroughly enjoyed the opportunity to use canoes. Apart from the short ride in the canoe from the airstrip where we had landed – the easiest way down river to our base – we had also used this form of transport on another day to travel to a neighboring small settlement further along the river. There had been no problem with this and I had thoroughly enjoyed the ride, so I could not understand why a dream with this content should be pervading my life.

However, I knew it was something I should not ignore, so to help me resolve it I telephoned John. The feeling that perhaps I should not be taking this trip was growing. As I explained my predicament he listened carefully, then suggested I should 'journey' and ask my spirit guides to help with an understanding.

This I did and the message was clear: I was not to take a ride in the dugout. No reason was given but the instruction was very precise. The way to get around this problem without forgoing the trip was also shown to me and it was very simple. When the plane dropped us off, I was to walk with the Shuar back to the camp along the trail that they use, a hike of about an hour but no great hardship. Also, if the group went by river using the canoes to visit other areas, I was to remain in the village of Miazal.

I was a little disappointed at missing out on my boat ride, yet consoled myself with the thought of still being able to go on the trip. The spirits gave me no explanation but there was no way I would disobey their instructions; I mentally accepted them, and from that moment the warning dreams ceased.

Once more I packed my case and before long was repeating the trip of six months ago – though these journeys can never really be repeated. The people are always different and the places might look the same but they never are. The situations that arise are also presented in accordance with that moment in time.

Again, because of the logistics of getting us safely in and out of the jungle, John had restricted the number of those who wished to come, so there were only twelve of us; even in such a small group there will be some people with whom you feel a great affinity and always at least one person who will 'press your buttons'. It is the latter who are our greatest teachers, for they disclose the imperfections in our own characters that we need to change most. It takes a very long time before we can accept that these people, who we feel are intruding on our lives, are in fact holding up a mirror for us.

We again visited the Tamayos at their home in the mountains and witnessed their dramatic fire-blowing healing methods, but although I knew I was privileged to be there, it was the latter part of the trip that again seemed to be calling me. I was impatient to get into the jungle.

There was a lot of hanging around at the airport, for the weather was very unpredictable and we were waiting for the clouds to lift. Because of the size of the group it was necessary for the small plane to make two trips and I was in the second half of the group to leave. My patience was tested as we kicked our heels at the airport, watching the slow gathering of the clouds that would keep us on the ground.

But finally we were out over the treetops, and before long the plane was bumping down on the rough grass runway. As the others made for the riverbank, I turned to greet one of the Shuar guides waiting to accompany me, and we began what I knew would be a very enjoyable walk to the village.

It felt like coming home. I was so much more comfortable in this part of Ecuador rather than on the mountains; there was no rational explanation for this, for the first part of the trip had been wonderful and fascinating, but this was what I had been waiting for: the coming few days were the reason I had returned.

On one of the days, we made an arduous and long trek up to a special point in the river where, side by side, two waterfalls drop into the river from hundreds of feet above. Although they fall only about fifty feet apart, these two cascades of water are very different: one is ice cold as it runs off the surface of a snow-covered mountain, whilst the temperature of the other is very warm, for it emerges from a lower point where there is activity from the internal volcanic area.

For me this was all part of my cleansing preparation, including the fasting on the following day, as I would once more be taking a measure of ayahuasca. I had never indulged in what is now termed 'recreational drug taking' and for me the use of what the Shuar refer to as the 'Sacred Vine' is far removed from this category. I approached my entry into this ritual with great respect and awareness. As well as the obligatory twenty-four hour fast, I felt the need to cleanse my body and take time to meditate, in order to empty my mind and focus on the night ahead.

The shaman who would be preparing the sacred potion, conducting the ceremony and performing the healings arrived in the morning, for the unique preparation and 'cooking' of the ayahuasca takes many hours. He had traveled for miles on foot, following tracks through the forest, and everyone was relieved to see him arrive safely as there had been torrential rain the previous night and the swollen rivers had made his passage very difficult. I was a little disappointed to see that it was not Daniel Watchapa, the shaman with whom I felt such an affinity, but I kept my feelings to myself and tried to follow the shamanic way of thinking that everything happens for a reason.

Before long we were gathered in the round house, the ayahuasca potion had been cooking under the close supervision of the male shaman, and once more I was mentally preparing myself. The shaman has a total understanding of the amount of brew to offer to each participant; he has already taken a small amount himself and is therefore open to be guided by the spirits. Not everyone on the trip will choose to enter the ritual and occasionally some will go through the fasting but then opt out at the last minute.

I was nervous and not looking forward to the period of purging, but was nevertheless prepared to accept this grueling physical aspect as a necessary part of the ritual. What I was waiting for with great anticipation was the journey that would follow, hoping that this time I would meet up with the giant anaconda. I swallowed the bitter brew and returned to my seat.

In time, I would learn that it is pointless to have expectations about the journey ahead or to dwell on what has happened on previous occasions, for each session is unique. This time, the Tibetan deity chose not to make his presence known, but as I sat there in the roundhouse, quietly and calmly waiting for the unavoidable purging to begin, I started to hear some unusual sounds.

The jungle is a very noisy place. Even without its human inhabitants, there was the constant sound of the river as it flowed past the camp, varying in intensity on an almost hourly basis. The air was filled with the call of myriad different birds, and added to this was the chattering communication of crawling, walking or climbing insects and animals that kept themselves hidden from sight. The creaking of trees, or the fluttering down of a dry leaf the size of a dinner plate, would add to the music.

But the sound I was hearing on this evening in the jungle was none of these. It was chanting. I could hear monks chanting and then the unmistakable sound of a gong being struck. It was a sound that was calling me; in fact it was summoning me.

I strained my ears. The sounds were unmistakable.

'Can you hear it?' I asked my companion.

'Hear what?' she replied.

'The chanting; the monks; the sounds,' I stated.

How could she fail to hear it? Where was it coming from? There was no mistaking it. I got to my feet to go in search of the source. I walked out of the round house and onto the path that headed just a few yards into the jungle.

But for me the jungle had disappeared. As I stepped outside the round house, the trees totally vanished; instead of walking along a dirt path, I saw a cobbled courtyard and felt myself walking across it. The clothes I had been wearing moments ago had also disappeared and I was now garbed in a saffron-colored robe which flapped against my legs. I glanced down and recognized the worn leather-strapped sandals on my dirty feet; through the thin soles I could feel the cobblestones.

There was a sense of urgency as I hurried across the uneven, uncovered area – the sounds reverberating through the air seemed to be calling me. It was a magnetic pull and it was coming from an area within the Buddhist temple complex where I now found myself. I was in a large open area with buildings on four sides; I had exited one part and was heading for the side directly opposite. As I moved, I felt the hot sun shining down on me. The courtyard was deserted, and as I scurried across I had the feeling I was late.

There was a familiarity about the scene, a sense that this was an act I had performed on numerous occasions. The building I was surrounded by was quite ornate and colored in rich reds, blues and gold with decorative trimming. A few steps ran almost the length of the part opposite me, the place I was headed for, and on this level was a long covered area with pillars; there was a sense that I was headed for a door on the right, underneath this portico.[3]

But I didn't get that far. A feeling of fear descended on me, a blanket of absolute terror. I knew I was about to face something so indescribably horrendous that I could go no further. It terrified me.

The scene disappeared and I fell into blackness. Then, with my heart still pounding, I found I was once more in the jungle and standing only a few yards from the round room. My physical body did not appear to have left this place, for my companion was saying, 'Wendy, wouldn't you prefer to go and sit down?'

I felt very distressed. As always, John was close at hand; his shamanic training and his natural instincts pick up emotions as surely as if he had visible antenna. I was not aware that I had said anything, and whatever my facial expression had divulged it was concealed, for the night was dark.

'I'm scared,' I stated. 'So scared.' Then I heard it again: once more came the clear sound of Tibetan chanting. I felt it calling me, sucking me back in. 'No!' I shouted. 'I can't go. I can't!'

John was very calm. 'Just take your time,' I heard him say.

'They're calling me – can't you hear them? You must hear it!' I demanded.

John is always supportive, but in his wisdom he knows that we each have our own journey and at the end of the day we are the ones who have to handle whatever presents itself. Whether he saw what I was seeing or heard what I was hearing, he didn't say. He knew it was my journey and my learning process.

'Just face it,' he said. 'See what it holds for you.'

Somewhere in my deepest subconscious I knew I had to go forward. To fail to do so would have left me with the deepest regrets. Whatever was about to happen was something I had to face and conquer.

Although I was terrified, I took a deep breath and surrendered into the sound, feeling myself being drawn back into my incarnation as a Tibetan monk. Once again the jungle and my companions vanished and I was alone, back in the temple confines, hurrying across the courtyard.

The fear hit me like a sledgehammer. I was holding down the screams that were trying to burst from my throat. I started up the three steps, my head pounding, not knowing my fate but aware that I was about to face unbelievable horror. I turned to the right and placed my hand on the door. I knew I had to enter, knew that a terrifying experience lay waiting for me in the room beyond, but I pushed myself forward – for I also knew that I had to continue this journey, whatever the fear.

In that moment everything vanished. The scene, the fear, all emotion and energy relating to it just disappeared in a trice. I was back in the jungle, feeling weak and exhausted, and my companions half-carried me to my bed. As I felt them lift my feet onto the bed and put a cover over me, I had a vision of the sky filled with hundreds of large black birds, cawing and wheeling around. This cleared and turned to darkness, then the scene with the birds briefly repeated itself, not once but twice more.[4]

The next thing I knew, I was waking up and it was daylight. There had been no meeting this time with the giant anaconda, no visit from the gorilla and no flying.

The vision and the shift to what I felt was a past life were indelibly etched into my mind.

I allowed myself to visualize the experience once more and it felt like confirmation of what I already believed to be true. As I viewed the temple and allowed the fear to briefly touch me again, there was a strong feeling that I knew exactly where I was, what my role in that lifetime had been and what I was about to witness. Deep within me, there was a positive realization that I had been the temple oracle in that particular lifetime as a Buddhist monk. What I had witnessed that day in my role as oracle had been the invasion of Tibet: I had foreseen the atrocities, the destruction and the annihilation of a beautiful culture. It seemed so far-fetched, but in my heart I knew it was the truth.[5]

My hope that the shaman would give me a helpful interpretation of my shift into what I felt certain was a past life was dashed, for when I told him about my vision and change of location he made no comment; he just looked at John and said, 'She has great *arutam*.' As for the meaning of the black birds, he conveyed that his feeling was that they were there to 'give me strength'.

The word *arutam* had also been used by Daniel Watchapa, and on my return home I searched for its meaning in every dictionary I could find, but all to no avail.

The images from the journey were so strong and so real that they remained very clear, and in the days following this trip I constantly tried to make sense of this vision – to discover what the teaching was – for I felt there was a powerful lesson to be learned. The only conclusion I arrived at was that fear itself is an illusion. If you can accept this and face your fears, confront them head on and find the courage to make a movement towards them, then they in turn will fade and disappear.

We returned to Cusco and, with only one day remaining before we left Ecuador, spent time with another shaman. This was the first South American female shaman I had met; her name was Maria Juana. She lived in a small village not far from the town of Cusco, holding her 'surgery' in a back room of her home. She was very well known and people traveled miles to see her.

It was here that I and several members of our group received an individual healing from her; mine proved to be rather interesting. Our interpreter, a man whom John has worked with for many years and who is now a close friend, told many stories about her as we waited. One thing he mentioned was that she worked closely with her spirit guide, who was a white dove.

The Ecuadorian shamans have no appointment system. For them, there is no such thing as being early or late; they believe everything happens at the right time, so they choose not to 'arrange' their days, simply allowing events to flow. We hung around for a long time, as it was three hours before Maria Juana arrived and quite some time after that before I finally got to have my healing. By this time, I had totally forgotten about the white dove.

It had been a full and exhausting ten days. I was hungry and my jet lag had caught up with me, leaving me feeling very tired. This tiny weather-beaten woman is very strong and she is a very 'hands-on' healer. It was when she was right in the middle of physically shaking me around that I 'saw' a white dove, in front of my eyes and very close to my face. Strangely, it didn't fly past but fluttered with wings outstretched, staying in one position in front of me with its tail down and underbelly exposed – an angle at which most birds do not hover, but there it was![6]

Chapter 11

FEARS AND THE FOURTH DIMENSION

The Dream Change organization had so far guided and served me well, and with their help my learning was progressing in leaps and bounds. This time, instead of a trip to another country, I booked myself onto a one-week workshop that John was facilitating in May 2000. Once more I made a transatlantic flight from Ireland to Miami and from there drove up to Palm Beach.

Again I was pushing myself out of the comfort zone and felt slightly anxious. I was still very new to Shamanism, and although I was keen to learn, I was also aware that the knowledge I had was minimal. In the overall scheme of things I still knew nothing and was lacking in self-confidence, so as I embarked on this program an overall feeling that I might be a little out of my depth hung over me. But I was determined to increase my knowledge, and the path I was following seemed to be well signposted.

The workshop was being held at a Catholic convent, a residence that had at one time been busy but now housed only a handful of nuns. To help provide an income, the main assembly room and accommodation were rented out on a weekly basis to suitable applicants. It was a beautiful location on the shore of one of Florida's inner lakes; the biggest building contained the meeting and dining rooms, and to one side were large gardens, mainly laid to lawn with a few areas of shrubbery. Set close to the water were several two-story blocks containing the single en-suite bedrooms. It was basic, but neat and clean.

There were about seventy of us present. John Perkins was leading the workshop and was assisted once more by Eve and another woman, Mary , whom I had not previously met. Also present this week were two of the shamans I had first seen at the

Omega Gathering the previous September: the Brazilian shaman named Ipupiara who works in partnership with his lovely Peruvian wife, Cleicha. They now both spent their time moving between their homelands and the USA, having taken on the huge task of sharing and spreading the ancient knowledge of their cultures. John had known them for several years, worked with them closely, and was a great admirer of their talent and the work they were doing.

Amongst those gathered here, I was the lone Brit, but some of those attending had come from almost as far, including one fellow from Hawaii. Americans are on the whole a friendly race, easy to talk to, and over the first couple of days I settled in and began to really enjoy the work.

Apart from my introduction to Shamanism in Ladakh and the brief opportunity to watch the shamans working at Omega, this was all new to me, and to enter into it so fully each day was very satisfying. At last I felt I had found my pathway; no longer was I floundering. Finally there was some direction and purpose to my long search, and it was very exciting.

John encouraged us to search for our dreams, for something that lies deep inside our hearts, something achievable – as distinct from a fantasy. Many of the participants were committed environmentalists, deeply concerned about the damage being inflicted on our planet and seeking a way to make our lives more sustainable. John led us through exercises designed to seek out our spirit guides, animal guardians and unseen helpers, and always these journeys were accompanied by drumming – a sound proven to aid in the shift to a deep level of consciousness. This man is a great story teller and his tales of the years he spent with the Shuar, witnessing and partaking in shamanic activity, held us enthralled.

,Each day was filled and intense, and we were also preparing for a ceremony to be held on the night of the May full moon. At this auspicious time, at 3.35am, the moon, earth and sun would be in direct alignment, and this event would herald the great Eastern celebration of the Buddha: Wesak, a day of supreme spiritual impact. This festival is not a commemorative celebration, but rather a present living event, a sacred ceremony which takes place each year involving Buddha, the Christ and the spiritual hierarchy, as a blessing is poured forth upon our planet. On this day, many of the spiritual structures in the East believe the forces of enlightenment flow outward into human consciousness.

I had no idea that this event would be taking place until after I had arrived and I puzzled over the synchronicity of it, for it was on the day of this same ceremony approximately one year ago – not the same calendar date but the time of the Wesak alignment – that I had been with Eve and John in Ladakh. This was the very same day that the three of us had sat at the feet of His Holiness the Dalai Lama, and the same day as my unexplained experience in the room of the Tibetan oracle Tsering Dolma.

I planned on setting my alarm so that I could be up and outside of my room, to sit and meditate in the moonlight at this special moment in time. One of the other women, whose name was Debbie and with whom I shared a table for meals, asked if I would knock on her door when I went out, as she would like to do the same.

When the alarm went off, I threw on some clothes and duly went first to her room, but her door had been left wide open and there was no sign of her or of anyone else.

It was a clear night and the glow from the moon lit the gardens; they seemed deserted. I walked to the side of the ocean, where I sat down, gazing at the beautiful reflection of the moon, and there I meditated for about an hour in total silence. I neither heard nor saw anyone, and when I passed Debbie's room on my way back to bed there was still no sign of her.

The following morning, we were all gathered in the meeting room, about to start work again, when Debbie burst into the room and, to our astonishment, started screaming and running around. John and Eve, along with a couple of people there who had medical training, managed to calm her and remove her from the room. It was necessary to have her hospitalized. Although Debbie did not admit to any psychiatric condition, the general consensus was that she had ceased taking her medication for a manic problem; at the time there was no proof of this, but her terror and panic were painful to witness and evoked much compassion from the group.

I volunteered with another woman to pack Debbie's belongings and clear her room, and later in the afternoon we went together to do this. Earlier in the week, Debbie had entered the conversation at the table and mentioned that she was a Catholic and had gone to mass in the convent chapel that morning; she told us how beautiful it had been. Now as we entered her room, we discovered that the two bibles that the Center placed in each room had been put at the back of the top shelf. The large crucifix – identical to those that hung in each bedroom – had also been removed from the wall and put into a cupboard.

I said nothing to my companion but I felt very uncomfortable: the energy in this room was very disturbing. She seemed oblivious to it and was chatting away, but for me there was a palpable sense of something dark. It was a bright sunny afternoon, but I took a deep breath and shuddered. My companion began collecting up the clothes and seemed unaware of anything out of the ordinary. As she left with a bag of Debbie's belongings, I made sure the door stayed wide open as I remained to strip the bed.

I did a last check and found only a small pair of tweezers, so I locked the room and took the key, relieved to be out of there. Nevertheless, just holding the key and tweezers made me feel uneasy and out of balance. I knew I had a 'black attachment': I was sensing something without form, but it was an evil presence.

I went to the reception area where I had registered on my arrival, to try and leave Debbie's room key, but it no longer existed – it had been manned by people from John's previous workshops who volunteered to do the paperwork; the nuns from the convent merely rented out the facilities and remained detached from any further involvement.

The sickening feeling that an evil presence was attached to me persisted, and once the sun had set it felt even worse. For so many years, I had had to handle and resolve the majority of my metaphysical experiences alone; there had rarely been anyone I could put my questions to, no one I felt I could trust or who would even understand. Therefore it never crossed my mind that John or Ipupiara or Cleicha would be familiar with such energies and be able to help me. Once again I felt this was something I had to handle alone.

I am sure no one looking at me had any idea of the trauma I was enduring during that evening. I found it impossible to eat any dinner as this bad, bad feeling persisted. Even the Chorten ceremony, which was beautiful and powerful and for which we had been preparing all week, did nothing to ease or release this terrifying, black, vampire-like attachment. All of these feelings I kept to myself, but that night, when the ceremony had concluded and I started to walk alone along the path to my room, I was so scared I felt sick.

Neither physical pain nor physically dangerous situations bother me. At various times in my life I have faced and overcome many emotionally difficult episodes, but whenever I feel this 'black energy', it has the ability to suck out and destroy all my courage; it really frightens me. Sitting like a great weight on my chest, the powerfulness of it fills me with terror – a profound fear that is hard to quell – and I dig deep into my boots to find the strength to cope with it. Somehow it never gets easier.

Once in my room, I put the lights on. The low-wattage bulbs did little to comfort me, but I put the tweezers and the keys to

Debbie's room on the floor just inside the door, as close to the outside as possible. I couldn't bear to have them any further into the room.

I got into bed and, at first, thought I would have to make a rapid exit from the room and go to sleep outside on one of the benches, for my stomach muscles contracted and a feeling of panic rose within me. Then, finding some deep resource of strength, I determined to confront my fear.

This lifetime is one of polarity and I believe that in order to experience the extreme moments of ecstasy, which has been my privilege, one must also face the other end of the scale; there has to be balance. As I lay in bed, I tried to recall each moment of every day throughout the workshop, to focus on the teachings and ceremonies of the week. Then I called on my spirit guides, requesting them to draw close and help me through the next few hours.

There was no specific spirit helper or deity, no image that I focused on as I called for aid, but to my amazement and relief a gorilla immediately appeared. It was a male gorilla – huge, absolutely enormous – and he was standing close to the door. Somehow I sensed that this was the same gorilla energy that had made such an impact on me during my ayahuasca journey. Now here he was – and such a powerful presence! By his side was a smaller version and I knew this was his female mate. Immediately my fear subsided; I closed my eyes and slept until 6.30am.

As I opened my eyes, I saw and felt that the room was clear: the dark power had vanished along with my gorilla guardians. I showered and dressed, and as I picked up Debbie's key and tweezers and left the room, I felt nothing.

The past twelve months, even considering it mildly, had been most unusual. After many years of jogging along, determined to follow my spiritual path in search of an understanding of that tumultuous six-week period that had changed my life, it seemed

I had reached a point where suddenly everything was accelerating. Deep down, I knew that all of this time I had been hoping for a recurrence: in spite of the trauma of that initial six-week experience, I wanted to relive it. But this time it was different, and although each non-physical experience had been new and intense, it seemed I was being given 'breathing space' in-between.

There was time to regain my balance. It was almost like leading a double life and I desperately needed both aspects of my existence. My quest had at times been exhilarating, but it had also been testing – summed up perfectly by an image given to me by my spirit guides during a meditation in this recent workshop: that of being swept up in a tsunami. In spite of continually having these extraordinary experiences, I had somehow managed to keep balanced, but I began to recognize that I was being guided through a minefield. I didn't understand why these events and dips into a non-physical realm were happening to me, but there was no doubt in my mind that they were orchestrated by the spirits, the gods and the ancestors.

Now my life began to fall into a pattern that would last for another few years. Like a pendulum, it would swing to extremes. There would be weeks when I went about my normal everyday life. Then, mostly without any warning, an inexplicable non-physical event would occur; always it would be something I had never heard or read about and something I was not searching for. But when it happened I would dutifully record it and always, always, there would come a time when I would either attend a workshop at which the speaker would share information on that particular phenomenon, or else I would read or hear of it in some other way.

Occasionally confirmation would come within days, but I also had to learn to be patient, for often it would be several years before I would discover some obscure book describing the same metaphysical circumstance. Only then would the disclosure seal my experience.

It was all a huge period of intense learning. Slowly my knowledge of the non-physical increased, and all the while I was slowly connecting to my true self. The façade that I had presented to the world was crumbling and my personality was changing; the anger that I had carried was dissipating and seemed to be replaced by a strength and confidence that I had been unaware I possessed.

My desire to understand more of this great universe of which we are a small but intricate part was unabated; I not only sought out workshops and trips but also simply followed my instinct. There seemed to be a well within me, a store of secret knowledge that I had tapped into, something that I was accessing. With this inner knowledge came positive guidance about the path I should follow to help me rediscover what I had learned eons ago.

Although I was excited and determined to learn as much as I could about Shamanism, I continued to explore other areas; my interest in Egypt and the affinity that I felt to that civilization remained strong. In September 2000 I attended a workshop facilitated by the ARE, the center that holds and promotes the works of Edgar Cayce. This weekend event, focusing on the mysteries of ancient Egypt, was to be held at Deerfield Beach, Florida and the main speaker would be John Van Auken.

My attention and thoughts were set on learning more about the multitude of gods and goddesses – visually depicted forms of divine energy – that were a prominent part of the lives of the ancient Egyptians, but once again a strong intervention by an unseen element would show in a powerful way how much they were already pervading my own life.

On the Friday evening as this weekend workshop commenced, I took my seat in the crowded auditorium. I had pencil and pad ready to record information and views from speakers who had spent the best part of their lives learning about the mysteries of this fascinating country, and I was totally unaware that before this weekend was over I would have taken a trip into what is referred to as the 'fourth dimension'. This was not a metaphysical experience that I was expecting, nor had I in any way explored this concept or sought out how to enter it. Even the phrase 'fourth dimension' was unfamiliar. I had no recollection of any talks or articles that would have focused on this subject, and no passing comment had ever aroused my interest.

My understanding at this stage of my knowledge was that there are many realms other than the physical; the fact that these exist totally unseen or recognized by our limited physical senses was now something I accepted and believed without reservation. I had personal experience that there is a non-physical world that we can access and that there is a dimension occupied by the spirits of those who have recently dwelt on the earth plane. The word 'recently' I use loosely, as time has an unquantifiable measure once we move from the physical.

My knowledge of the various levels of conscious awareness was acquired mostly by my own out-of-the-ordinary experiences, augmented by reading at a basic level to ensure comprehension. These other realms I had neatly categorized into groups as an aid to my understanding. I had many personal experiences of these extra levels of consciousness beyond the normal usage, but to enter dimensions even beyond this was stretching me yet further.

There is a saying: 'When the pupil is ready, the teacher will appear'. True to this, although each new metaphysical experience came unexpectedly and as a complete surprise, there was always a rest period in-between that helped me assimilate it.

The seminar was entitled 'Ancient Mysteries' and was being held in a beachfront hotel where I had a room on the eighth floor, overlooking the ocean. The first evening was devoted to the understanding of the kundalini, the force that the Indians call *prana* and which is also referred to as *chi*. The speaker impressed on us the importance of allowing this life force to flow without restriction through the seven chakras – our energy centers. It is the flow of this energy that gives us the ability to raise our level of consciousness; on this higher level we are able to unite our souls with the spirit of god, and in this joining we can find oneness with the creator.

This for me was familiar territory, but the magic of such knowledge never diminishes. John Van Auken was immensely knowledgeable, funny and perfectly in balance and harmony with both the physical and spiritual aspects of himself. He produced many biblical quotes and stories that, when interpreted, were confirmations of the need to raise our minds to a higher level in order to access the link between our physical and spiritual selves. His talk was illustrated with slides of Egyptian tomb pictures showing the winged serpent, the symbol of the kundalini: it portrays the rising up of this coiled energy that then takes flight.

We finished the evening with a meditation and the instruction to remember our dreams that night, as the first session the following morning would start with a dream analysis. My plan was to take an early morning walk along the beach before breakfast, so with this in mind I was in bed by 10.30pm, preparing for sleep.

As I put the light out, I remembered an occasion several years earlier in Sikkim, a province in northern India, where I had been attending a Kala Chrakra initiation led by the Dalai Lama. At the conclusion of one of the days, His Holiness had instructed us to have a prophetic dream. He had told us exactly how to position our bodies as we lay in bed – a position we were told would aid in our ability to achieve this task. This memory popped into my thoughts as I lay there in my Florida hotel room, and I adjusted my body into the recommended form.

I slept well, but dreamlessly. It was daylight when I awoke. I got out of bed and looked out of the window. Here on the eighth floor, where only the birds might avail themselves of a peek through the windows, I had left the curtains pulled back. It was a stormy day; it had been raining heavily, and low black clouds were scudding across the sky.

The sea was very rough; large waves curled over and hit the sand. No one was out walking on the beach this morning. As I looked, I saw an enormous tree stump about to be washed up; it was floating like a large round boat and appeared to be the discarded, sawn-off part of a giant redwood tree. The waves were propelling it rapidly towards the shore. I'd never seen anything like it. I called my husband to wake up and come and watch, but he slept on.

As this huge piece of timber finally settled onto the beach, the waves continued to crash over it, dragging the sand from around its sides, setting it firmly in place. Again and again the water swept over it, the sand sieving and shifting, and with every wave it sank deeper and the hold on it from the land grew ever firmer.

I needed to go down and watch this more closely, so without stopping to get dressed I quickly left the room. For some reason, I chose to use the stairs instead of the elevator, and as I hurried down, I looked out of the window on the stairwell and saw to my dismay that the storm had created an extra high tide; the sea had fed further inwards and was now lapping around the side of the building. As I continued walking down, I became aware that my feet were getting wet and to my horror saw that water was now running down the stairs.

My first thought was that the tail-end of a hurricane had passed through during the night and the accompanying rainfall had found its way inside the building.

I reached the ground floor foyer and happened to glance through the glass walls into the restaurant as I passed. What I saw there stopped me in my tracks. My three children, their partners and my grandson were all in there! I did a double take. Questions flashed through my mind: *Has Barry brought them all out as a surprise for me? Do I have a special birthday or special anniversary?* But I knew the answer was 'No'. *They can't be here*, I thought. *I must be dreaming. But I'm not. Or am I?*

I knew I wasn't. I knocked on the glass, but it made no sound and no one looked in my direction. It was the strangest feeling. While an inward part of me was saying, *This isn't possible; you have to be dreaming,* the physical aspect of this experience was so multidimensional that it was incredibly difficult to persuade myself that I was in a dream. There in the foyer of the hotel, with seemingly normal activity going on, I stood: an invisible observer.

I was on the verge of panicking, for although I felt no different, I knew that to everyone else I was invisible. They could neither see nor hear me. I needed to find the path back to 'normality'. Instantly, I knew I had to remain calm and in control, in order to decide what to do. I could feel my heart pounding, but logically I decided the solution was to retrace my steps, return to bed and re-enter the sleep state.

With a last glance at my family, I turned and proceeded back up the stairs, noting as I did so that the water was starting to recede. I climbed the stairs, passing each level until I arrived at the eighth floor, and walked along the corridor, seeing no one. Coming to the door with our room number on it, I stood outside.

Then, without any consideration or hesitation, I walked *through* the door, straight into the bedroom. Swiftly I slipped into bed and instantly resumed the sleep state.

I awoke. The knowledge of what had happened instantly flooded my mind. Very cautiously and slowly, I opened my eyes and saw that it was light. Morning sunshine was filtering into the room. My husband was up and making tea.

With some trepidation, I eased myself out of bed and walked towards the window. I looked out; down below me all seemed normal; there were a handful of people out walking on the beach. There was no sign of the tree stump. The sea was calm, and gentle waves lapped the shore.

The clarity of the night's events was too sharp to be dismissed. I sat back on the side of the bed, feeling decidedly 'wobbly'. Once again a non-physical experience had arrived with its usual omission of any warning announcement. This time it had left me physically depleted. I looked at the clock; it was past eight. I had slept for ten hours. I couldn't remember the last time I had slept so long.

I had a quick cup of tea and a shower, and then departed to the meeting room, looking the part of the interested student – my physical appearance belying the internal confusion. I walked into the hall with the old familiar feeling that I had a foot in both worlds.

Later in the day, when the opportunity arose, I briefly described the previous night's experiences and asked John Van Auken, the respected director of the ARE, if he could give me an explanation. His honest response was that he felt it was a momentary shift into the fourth dimension.

Chapter 12

THE JOURNEY CONTINUES

This is the way my life progressed. One moment I would be having the most extraordinary experiences; then it was back to everyday reality with a bump, and my days would continue on a pleasant but mundane level.

It was a huge learning period. After each of these events, I would try to recall every detail of it; I would go through a process of reliving it and then trying to make some sense of it, finding a reason and a way to understand it all. Every time, I would try to record the events as honestly as I could, without adding anything or embellishing it in any way.

Many times during the lull, I would seek out the metaphysical and take myself off to a sacred spot: to standing stones if I was in Ireland; to Glastonbury and the surrounding area if I was in England; and to a church or cathedral if I was in another city. Always on these occasions, I would simply sit down and meditate. I gave up trying to deliberately shift myself into another realm, because it never happened.

As I moved through such days without any connection to the metaphysical (I called them 'the ordinary periods' and they often stretched into several months), I would feel as if a huge part of me had absented itself. I wondered if it had all ended. I would grow concerned that there would be no more metaphysical experiences, that my previous time had been my last, and now it was all over.

The thought of no longer having a connection to other realms was distressing; indeed the idea of having to spend the rest of my life devoid of this powerful part of my life was almost too much to bear. But although, so far, I have never been able to make the shift purely by choice, it never has ended. Always, after a time period of varying length, another non-physical experience would occur, different from the last; and gradually I tentatively accepted that the metaphysical would never leave. Even if it did, I persuaded myself, I had enough memories to keep me going for the rest of my life.

I finally came to realize that these periods of 'normality' were an important and necessary part of my life and that they were needed in order to keep my feet on the ground, to maintain a balance and hold on to my sanity.

Somewhere in the back of my mind I knew that there was more than a personal reason for my experiences to continue to occur; I sensed that one day in the future they would serve to help many others. My experiences would, I felt, provide assistance to many people brought up in the Western world and indoctrinated into our science-based culture – the very same people who would soon experience such phenomena for themselves, as the expected and long-predicted rise in consciousness begins. This rise has been forecast by a great many prophets and foretellers from various ancient cultures.

The remainder of the year 2000 I spent in England, quietly getting on with my life, checking out the variety of websites that were popping up, and doing a lot of reading. Although my main search was centered on Shamanism, I was open to anything that crossed my path as my search continued.

It was after reading some of Michael Harner's books that I found the Sacred Trust website in Cornwall. This UK offshoot of his American base offered a selection of workshops and I enrolled for a preliminary two-day introduction to Shamanism, to be held in London and led by Simon Buxton. The first day was run on similar lines to the events that John Perkins had facilitated: we did journeying to the sound of drumming, retrievals of spirit tools, and listened as he guided us through the basic shamanic beliefs and practices. It was on the second day, as we were preparing to enter another journey, that I was given yet another gift.

There were about sixty people present: the usual cross-section of males and females of all ages and from all walks of life. The building we met in was next to the river and had probably originally been a warehouse; our meeting room on the first floor was rectangular in shape, and large windows that let in plenty of light ran along one of the shorter walls. We were all seated on the floor and I was beneath one of the windows, almost in the corner. From where I was sitting, the door leading into the room was at the far end from me on the right-hand wall that ran towards my corner.

Simon and his assistant were seated about halfway along the left-hand wall, with the rest of us spread out, sitting comfortably on the floor; those without back jacks had either cushions or chairs placed close to the walls.

We were into the final afternoon session; Simon had been talking for about half an hour, answering questions and allowing the theme to run through various areas of discussion. The re-emergence of an interest in Shamanism in my home country was very much in its infancy, and although our instructor was enthusiastic and honest, he was also guarded in his information – and rightly so, for the uncovering of some of these ancient beliefs and practices is anathema to many people indoctrinated into our Western Christian culture.

Then, to my astonishment, as I was calmly sitting there listening, I saw a huge black panther enter the room – apparently through the door. He was male and, although fully grown, was not quite mature. The only word to describe him is *magnificent*. His coat was so sleek that it looked as if it had been polished, for it had a sheen that rippled over his frame as he slowly walked forward. His paws were large and supple, and the lower joint allowed them to bend back to a sharp degree as he picked them up and then seemed to flip them out in front of him as his leg went forward to take another step. I was transfixed and could not move my eyes from him.

He moved in front of the people seated at the far end of the room opposite me, and slowly but purposely walked across from the door towards the left-hand side of the room. Here he half-turned and headed along that side. He was walking close to the people but ignoring them all, looking to neither right nor left.

I knew he was heading for me. *The quickest way,* I thought, *would have been to come from the door straight along the right-hand wall* (logic was penetrating this vision), but in spite of this I knew for certain that he was coming to me.

Skeptics would call this 'imagination', but what is imagination? It is just a word our culture uses to describe something that none of our five physical senses are registering. I could see this panther as clearly as if I had been using my eyes – indeed this sixth sense had even sharper vision – but there was no reaction from my companions so I assumed they were not aware of him.

The big cat continued his rhythmic and stealthy walk, going past Simon and his assistant, then on to the corner of the room on my left. He walked purposefully, all the while holding his head steady; his eyes looked straight ahead, not once glancing to either side. At the same time, he still kept close to the seated participants. Then, without cutting the corner, he again did the half-turn and came along towards me. My eyes had not left him since the moment he had so unexpectedly entered the workshop and I am sure my jaw hung loose, leaving my mouth open. As he reached me, he stopped. His rear end dropped; I swear I felt the floor creak as he flopped himself down right in front of me. He had his back to me and lay at an angle to the room, with his rear quarters resting on his right haunch and both of his front legs stretched out in front of him. His neck and head he held upright, and from this position he surveyed the room.

The sun shone through the windows onto his smooth, gleaming coat and there was a slightly earthy smell to him. To me he was bodily there. A veil had lifted, and his world and mine had merged. I experienced no fear and was oblivious to all else in the room, just watching in wonder as his flanks rose and dipped with his breathing.

Then Simon's voice cut into my thoughts and I heard him say, 'What we are going to do next is take a journey to find our animal spirit guide.'

Mine was one step ahead and had already introduced himself! I lay down and stretched out, taking care to keep my legs well to the side of my welcome guide.

The drumming started and my inner vision was filled with the head of the panther: a close-up of his face, with his eyes staring at me. His eyes were of an amazing color: neither green nor gold, but somehow a combination of the two. I cannot remember any message or specific communication, just this totally consuming gaze that sucked me in.

But then it suddenly vanished. It didn't fade away; one moment it was there – in front of me, the head of a living, breathing panther – and the next moment it was gone. Within seconds I heard the tempo of the drumming change to a constant and rapid beat, followed by four very loud single beats which signaled the end of the journey.

I opened my eyes and sat up. My panther had vanished. After what had been at least fifteen minutes, how had he known that within a fraction of that time Simon would signal that it was time to end the journey? How had he known it was time to leave just moments before the drumming changed?

How had I known he would stop when he reached me? And why had he walked around the room the way he did, when there was a much quicker route straight along the right-hand wall from the door to me? It is logical questions like these that always arise in my mind yet somehow constantly confirm the existence of the 'other reality' and its connection to me.

In the months that followed, I was often aware of this

handsome animal guide, although occasionally I would get sucked into a rationalist way of thinking and put it all down to what our culture describes as a 'figment of the imagination'.

By the early part of 2001 I was beginning at last to find a confidence in my beliefs. My family was wary and I had learned what I could share with them and what would strain their sensibilities. I would go to dinner parties and put on another face; often it seemed to me that I was two people, but now I was careful to protect what I sensed was the 'real me', so I felt no obligation to attend events that my gut feeling warned me to avoid.

The synchronicities abounded – they came almost daily – and it seemed as if the spirits were playing delightful tricks on me. I recorded them all in my journal and some were far beyond the odds of normal possibilities.

It took another workshop organized by the Dream Change Coalition in May 2001 to enforce my belief in myself as a shaman and to accept that often I see through a window into a different dimension. It is a blessing to have received this reassurance, for I battle constantly with the Catholic dogma that was enforced on me throughout my childhood. Attendance at this further workshop sealed my total acceptance and appreciation for the panther that is one of my spirit guides.

It was around this time that I began to sense a feeling of restlessness within me; it had been over ten years since I had commenced my search into the paranormal which had led me to the spiritual side of life. There was a growing awareness that all I was experiencing and had learned was for a reason, but there was no task I felt inspired to do. It wasn't that I didn't have the time or inclination; I simply was not drawn to any particular healing modality.

A week spent back at the convent in Palm Beach would prove to be a major shape-shift for me. A large percentage of the attendees arrived on the Sunday evening, ready for the start of the convention at 9.00am the next morning. Although I could have driven up early on the first morning, I too preferred to be there the day before.

Our accommodation was ready, but the food facilities would not be available until the next day, so a large group of us met and walked out to a nearby restaurant. As we stood there in line, introducing ourselves, chatting and waiting to be seated, I suddenly knew I would have to leave. The noise, the people – everything seemed to be crowding in on me, and the inside voice was screaming, *Get out of here!*

I was feeling 'tender': every one of my senses seemed to be on red alert. I had by now learned to listen to my feelings and respond to them, so I knew I had to leave immediately. I made my excuses and beat a swift retreat, returning to the convent, where I carefully avoided the few people who were around and happily spent the rest of the evening alone. As I prepared for bed, I jotted a note in my journal: 'My neck feels odd!'

It was on the first day, within the first couple of hours, that I found wonderful confirmation that my panther spirit guide was more than just my imagination. The numbers attending this type of workshop are growing, and on this day there were close to ninety of us. After John Perkins had given his introductions and spoken a little about Shamanism, we settled down to start work.

The first task was to participate in what is known as a 'cleansing ceremony'; for this you sit opposite a partner and for a few minutes visualize them engulfed in one of the elements. It is as simple as that. First we were told to turn and find a partner, someone we didn't know; this was easy, for most people following a shamanic path find it to be a solitary journey and many who attend these events come alone. At these workshops, we learn together, bond and share experiences. Then we each return to our individual communities, finding that only rarely do our paths cross again.

I exchanged names with the woman sitting next to me, with whom I was to share this ritual. She confided that this was her first workshop and that everything was very new to her.

We duly completed the cleansing ritual, and the class was allocated a few minutes for each person to exchange stories with their partner and relate their experience.

It was my partner's afterthought that stunned me, for here was a person whom I had never seen before this morning and with whom I had exchanged only first names. After sharing with me her shamanic journey and the element that had prevailed during the spiritual cleansing, she added, 'It was very odd when we first started. You know, when I first closed my eyes, and before the visualization of the element started, I felt a large animal pass between us. I actually felt him brush past and I know it was a panther. It was so real! I was too scared to open my eyes. I've never had any experience like this. What do you think it means?'

Events such as this continue to reinforce my belief in an unseen world.

I immersed myself in the workshop. Each day, I reveled in the rituals and journeys, and loved hearing the sound of the drums; I was finding great satisfaction in the process of learning. Ipupiara and Cleicha, the husband-and-wife team of shamans that I had witnessed working at the Omega Institute and had been present the previous year, were here again to assist and teach, and also to offer individual healings.

When John had introduced this lovely couple to the assembled gathering on our first morning, Ipupiara had shared an account of a time when Christian missionaries had first come to his remote home in the jungle many years before. When the priests told the tribespeople the story of Jesus raising Lazarus from the dead, one of the men from the nearby village had responded by saying, 'Ah, yes. Our shaman did that last week.' Later, I took the opportunity to share with him my own Lazarus story.

This year I availed myself of the opportunity to have a private individual healing with the Brazilian shaman and his wife. The focus of their combined energies and love provided a strong cathartic cleansing and I found myself weeping gently. They gave me instructions that when I returned home I was to light a large green candle; this, they said, would complete the healing. The next week, following this direction, I duly went to a local store and purchased a strong green candle. I was amused later that day as I lit it, for I saw on the side of it a picture of a man that I had not noticed when I bought it. And underneath it was written his name: 'St Lazarus.'

At the workshop we were kept very busy throughout the week, but I was aware of great changes going on within me, both in my physical body and emotionally. I was also having potent dreams that I knew were symbolically representing a huge shift in my personal relationships.

Physically, odd things were happening, for although I felt fit and well, I seemed to have lost my appetite. At one point I tried to persuade myself to eat, but the food got stuck in my throat; it wasn't sore but I just seemed unable to swallow anything. My sense of smell, which is always acute, was heightened. There was an instance when one woman stopped to speak to me and I had to take two steps backwards; although at that point she was not smoking, I knew that sometime within the last couple of hours she had been, and the smell of it lingering around her nauseated me.

For two nights running, I woke up in the early hours with a strange headache. There was a core of pain right in the center of my forehead, as if there was a hole burning there; I placed a wet cloth across it and within minutes the pad was hot. As I ran my hand across it in the dark, I could feel the patch of heat: incredibly my fingers could trace the outline of a two-inch diameter circle of pure heat, burning its impression into the cold flannel.

It came to Thursday morning. All week we had been

preparing ourselves to move forward in our lives, to find our mission, to discover what our hearts were telling us. Now was the time to leave all past pain behind and to step forward, facing the future with vigor and commitment, walking with a new and positive approach to our lives. John prepared us to take a journey. Giving instructions to seek out the 'snake energy', he urged us to find and identify with this force and use it to empower ourselves.

For thousands of years and in all ancient cultures, the snake has been a constant symbol. Artifacts dating back many thousands of years indicate that both the bird and the snake were important symbols from the earliest times. The high priestess or shaman was also often represented as an anthropomorphic representation of a bird or snake – a reptile that has always been recognized as a source of powerful energy. An example is the Hermes staff with the two intertwined snakes which is used as the symbol of the medical profession.

Understanding John's message to visualize the snake as a sign that we were shedding our old persona and embracing a new path, we focused on the next ritual. There were over eighty of us attending this workshop, but we all found enough space and lay down comfortably on our backs on the floor of the main hall. John commenced the drumming, his beats joined by the sound of the drums of four other facilitators who were assisting at the event.

I lay there feeling the vibrations from the drumming flow through me, but my visualization, normally so vivid, was missing. The screen inside my head was blank; I couldn't seem to move my thoughts from the room. The drumming continued, but still there was nothing. I remained aware that I was lying on the floor in the work room and I could not produce any mental picture. This had never happened before, and as the minutes ticked by, I was unsure of what to do because, however hard I tried, there was still nothing.

Then there was a subtle yet distinct shift in my consciousness, and from the depths of my memory came the visions from my first ayahuasca-aided journey nearly two years before. Suddenly I was back in the rainforest, following a path, the same trail where the giant anaconda skin had been laid out. I was there in the rainforest; it was so real – the distinctive smell, the humidity and the whole feeling of the place. I was slowly walking back down that same single-file path, a path I recognized instantly.

I got to the place where the skin had been, and I stopped. The skin was no longer there!

As I stood there unmoving, I knew the anaconda was around. She was very, very close. Through every sense and every pore, I knew this; I felt her presence.

There were no visible signs of her. The forest, normally alive with sound, was unnaturally quiet – no movement from the trees or plants. Not a leaf rustled. But she was there.

In that instant, I instinctively knew that to hunt for her would be in vain, that I had to wait for her to come to me. I knew she was in the undergrowth on my left. Quietly I sat down on the opposite side of the path with my back against a tree and waited.

I heard the rapid drumbeat coming from the facilitator's drums – the sign to begin our return to a normal level of consciousness, to return to awareness of the workshop room – and I experienced a flash of disappointment that once again the anaconda had not arrived.

Then the first big beat of the drum came, the first of four loud single beats that were John's signal to end the journeying. In time with that one sound, vibrating and somehow hovering between the Ecuadorian rainforest and a convent in Palm Beach, I saw the anaconda. She suddenly appeared, rising up on the other side of the path directly opposite me. She was a truly giant snake, but with a speed that was astonishing she suddenly reared her head and lunged at me with her jaws stretched wide. In a split second she had swallowed me. Feet first, I slid into her until I was totally engulfed, my body suspended inside her, my head remaining inside her head.

I lay there dazed; then, as if in the far distance, I was vaguely aware of the workshop room. I could hear John's voice dimly talking to the other attendees. I was aware of their movements, of people sitting up. But I couldn't move. I was in no discomfort but feeling physically paralyzed.

The thought, *I am inside a snake*, filled my head. I opened my eyes – thankfully my eyelids worked. But they were the only part of my body that seemed to be under my control. My eyes looked straight up at the ceiling. It seemed that the snake's head was over my head; the rest of my body was inside the giant anaconda. There was a strange process of thought going on: a sense of relief that my eyes were lined up with the snake's eyes and that I could see.

Then a wave of panic swept over me as I thought, *What if everyone goes home and I'm left here inside the snake?* I couldn't speak; I couldn't move. The only faculty that remained was my ability to blink. I still had my sight, but that was fixed firmly on the ceiling.

The voices of the others sharing a description of their journeys drifted in and out. I noted the sensation that, when I blinked my eyes, it didn't feel like a regular blink. It was a strange sensation and one part of my brain equated it to the same process that a snake uses to clean the eyes – more of a sideways blink. It was all very bizarre.

At some point, there came an invisible connection with John and the thankful but unspoken realization that he was aware that something was happening to me; he knew something very strange was going on and that I hadn't just fallen asleep! He made no comment nor did he come in my direction. It was truly extrasensory communication.

Somewhere into my awareness came the memory of a fact: we were only halfway through this ritual journey; the second half would resolve my predicament. This thought came as a salve.

There was no indication of how it would be resolved; it seemed unimportant, for at this moment in time I was inside a snake. I could go no further than that.

Throughout the past minutes – I guessed it had been about ten or fifteen – I knew I had not moved a muscle, apart from blinking. Now I heard John give the instruction for everyone to lie back down and prepare to resume their journey.

The drumming started. Immediately my eyes closed and, within seconds, I experienced extreme physical feelings. There came a tightness in my torso; it was strongest in my chest and it grew in intensity. There was a desire to push, to push upwards towards my head. Then came contractions, like childbirth in reverse. There was a feeling of an immense pressure clamped around my lungs – it was restricting my breathing and I knew I had to push out of it. The drums were beating around me, louder and louder.

Then I felt my mouth opening. It opened wide, then even wider, stretching to its extreme. I was gasping for air as the tightness constricted me. Then, with one last push, I escaped; I felt myself emerge.

I was free, but exhausted. I rolled over onto my stomach and as I did so, there was a sensation of my skin painlessly splitting. This truly physical feeling started at the throat, ran down through the middle of my chest, over my abdomen and along the rest of my torso. I lay there, tremors passing through me, breathing deeply, and gradually the shaking ceased and my breathing returned to its normal level.

In time, I rolled again onto my back, but that was all – I was totally spent and unable to move. I knew I was out of the snake and back to Wendy, but I lay quite still with my eyes closed as the rest of the class continued their journey.

The sound of the drums signaled the session was finished. Slowly I opened my eyes and sat up; it felt as if I was coming out of a dream.

John looked around the room and asked, 'Anyone want to share their journey?' A few people were keen to do so, anxious to have John's input into their own interpretation.

Quiet then descended on the room. John took a deep breath, waved his hand to include the other facilitators who were seated beside him, and said, 'What we have seen today has been truly amazing. The snake energy was so powerful. In this room, we have just witnessed two shape-shifts.'

He looked to the other side of the room. 'Amy was frightening! She was really on the attack. Brian was drumming right beside her when she rose up and started to lunge at him.' He looked inquiringly towards one of the facilitators sitting next to him.

'I was scared – I don't mind admitting it,' answered Brian.

'Can you believe it?' continued John. 'This man is ex-SAS; he was a mercenary; he's a martial arts expert. That's how real and powerful this snake energy is. It transforms the person.'

Then John looked towards me. 'This side of the room, there was something equally amazing happening. The rest of us witnessed a cellular shape-shift. Wendy's face was overlaid by that of a snake.' To hear him say this was, for me, unbelievable. I had not spoken a word and here was confirmation of all I had experienced. He went on: 'At one stage, her mouth opened so wide that her jaw appeared to be dislocated! Eve, Mary and I all witnessed it.'

The eyes of everyone in the room turned in my direction.

'Would you mind sharing your sensations and thoughts with us all, Wendy?' requested John.

I acquiesced. Although I had returned from the altered state of consciousness, my senses seemed to be dulled, but I was able and pleased to have the opportunity to verbally record this awesome experience.

The week's workshop finished the following day, and the next night I had a very strange dream. I continue to refer to it as a 'dream' because it happened during the night when I was in the sleep state, but it was also much more.

I woke up. It was still dark and I didn't check the time, for as I lay there, I felt my body expelling an oil-like secretion; it was emitting from every pore and there was a bitter odor to it. I shot to wakefulness and ran my fingers over my body, expecting them to slide on an oily surface. But there was nothing.

I lay still, trying to assimilate my thoughts, but there was no explanation. However, my inner feelings left me in no doubt that it was in some way connected to the shape-shift into the snake. Once again I had experienced the extraordinary.

I returned to England for just a week, and to help get myself grounded I focused on some basic tasks, one of which was to sort through a large amount of furniture and artifacts that had been in storage for a couple of years. Whilst doing this, I was given a powerful lesson that my spirit guide panther had been in my life longer than I realized; this now remains as a constant reminder.

To my astonishment, when I was sorting through a stack of pictures, I came across a painting of a beautiful large black panther. I could remember buying it. I remembered being in the auction room, waiting for this lot to come up after previously seeing the picture and thinking I *must* have it. It really was the last thing I needed, for our large manor house was already on the market, but it called out to me and I knew that if I didn't buy it I would forever regret it. Shortly after this, we moved from our house in England, so the picture had never been hung on a wall; it had gone directly into storage and I had totally forgotten about it.

Following this find, I spent one month in Ireland trying to collate the shape-shift experience and my recollection of all the mysterious and powerful events that had entered my life over the past few years. I pulled them out of my memory and retrieved them. Rereading notes from my journals, I faced the experiences again and relived them all. At times my courage was severely tested.

Our culture finds such happenings unacceptable and I knew the revelation of such events would have some people questioning my sanity. I was balancing on the tightrope again. There was an undeniable reality as I reviewed each momentous milestone and this made it difficult to retain the stability needed to execute normal activities. It was an uphill task I faced: to find the ability to accurately and honestly record my impressions.

Many of the ancient prophecies were now coming to fruition and our world was changing rapidly. Deep inside me, I knew the time had come to disclose and share some of these experiences. I had to stand up and be counted.

Notes

1. Many years later, when technology had progressed at an unbelievable speed, there was a medical program on TV and I happened to glance at the screen when a film was being shown recording an endoscope as it was guided through the intestine. It was the same journey that I had made through the body, and I was rendered speechless as I witnessed a replay of exactly what I had seen many years before. Yet, however wonderful this new technology is, it failed to capture the intensity of the beauty that is within us.

2. Alternative healers talk about 'removing blockages' to attain a healthy mind and body. This, they claim, allows energy to flow smoothly between the chakras. In the same vein, shamans talk about removing 'the stone' to allow healing to commence.

3. Several years later, I was thumbing through a large illustrated book on Tibet by Michael Willis when my skin started to tingle, for before my eyes was a picture of the very temple I had seen in the vision. Its name is Dolma Lhakhang and it has a close association with Tara and the Maha Kala; by the time I saw this picture, both of these powerful deities were playing a prominent role in my life.

4. I have an apartment in Miami in a building situated at the water's edge; boat docks marked by wooden posts adjoin the garden. As I arrived back from Ecuador, I had a strange greeting: on not just one, but on every single post, was seated a large black bird.

5. Seven years after first reading Michael Willis' book on Tibet, even more parts of the jigsaw came together. By this time, the Maha Kala had on many occasions used my physical body to channel healing energies and he would also leave prophecies in my head. As I looked again at the book containing the picture of Dolma Lhakhang, I noticed on the preceding page

an image of the Maha Kala, and I realized it was this deity that had been calling me, as a Buddhist monk, to the temple that day. In that temple, I would have shape-shifted and become the oracle.

The caption to his picture reads: 'Maha Kala holds, in the crooks of his arms, the long wooden sounding board used to summon monks to assembly. This symbolizes Maha Kala's vow to protect all Buddhist monasteries.' Eventually, if you wait long enough, everything becomes clear.

6. Maria gives her clients a three-day prohibition after she has performed a healing. She provides strict instructions that you are to eat no fish, no pork, no onions or spicy food, and you are also forbidden to shower. Back in my Miami apartment on completion of the trip, I emerged from a wonderful hot shower the moment the three-day ban finished, and was standing with a towel wrapped around me. I looked out of the full-length bedroom window and there, strutting up and down on the terrace, seven floors up, was something I had never seen before. It was a white dove. It remained for about ten minutes; then, with a flap of the wings, it took off and never returned.

BOOKS

O is a symbol of the world, of oneness and unity. In different cultures it also means the "eye," symbolizing knowledge and insight. We aim to publish books that are accessible, constructive and that challenge accepted opinion, both that of academia and the "moral majority."

Our books are available in all good English language bookstores worldwide. If you don't see the book on the shelves ask the bookstore to order it for you, quoting the ISBN number and title. Alternatively you can order online (all major online retail sites carry our titles) or contact the distributor in the relevant country, listed on the copyright page.

See our website www.o-books.net for a full list of over 500 titles, growing by 100 a year.

And tune in to myspiritradio.com for our book review radio show, hosted by June-Elleni Laine, where you can listen to the authors discussing their books.

mySpiritRadio